IS DIVORCE THE ANSWER?

Irish Law of Torts, 1981 (with Bryan M.E. McMahon)
Casebook on the Irish Law of Torts (with Bryan M.E. McMahon)

William Binchy

Is Divorce the Answer?

AN EXAMINATION OF NO-FAULT DIVORCE
AGAINST THE BACKGROUND OF THE IRISH DEBATE

IRISH ACADEMIC PRESS

This book was printed in Ireland for
Irish Academic Press, Kill Lane,
Blackrock, County Dublin.

ISBN 0-7165-0314-X

Binchey, William
  Is divorce the answer?
  1. Divorce — Ireland
  I Title
  306.8'9'09417   HQ878

  ISBN 0-7165-0314-X

Contents

CHAPTER 1

The Divorce Debate

A 'divorce debate' has begun in Ireland. Not surprisingly, it has raised some passion but, so far, the discussion has tended to be much more a matter of slogans than of well-researched analysis. What follows is designed to assist the discussion by a detailed examination of the issues.

This analysis is limited to the issues of social policy. The religious area, where, of course, some important, but different, arguments may arise, I leave to others.

The humanitarian argument for divorce

A strong humanitarian argument can be made for divorce. It is easy to think of cases where divorce would appear to be not only a satisfactory solution, but, indeed, the *most desirable* solution. A woman may have been deserted by her husband, who has left her with young children to rear. She meets and falls in love with a man who is anxious to marry her and to take over the responsibilities of step-parent to her children. The children like the man very much. Would not divorce in such a case be a humane and sensible answer?

Other cases readily come to mind. A young married woman who has been battered by her husband returns to her home town. Is she to remain in the 'limbo' state of seperated wife for the next fifty years until his death? Or a couple who marry too young gradually grow apart from each other as they mature. While both do their best to live with each other, they find this impossible and separate by consent. Are they to be denied a second chance because, the argument goes, divorce is generally unacceptable to the community as the solution to marital problems? The core of the argument in favour of divorce is essentially humanitarian and caring. It calls on members of our society who are fortunate enough to belong to stable families to sympathise with, and to understand and respect, the position of those who are less fortunate.

But if the plea is basically a humanitarian one, the actual case for divorce is not self-evident. What seemed to be the best solution for certain cases in other countries resulted in quite alarming consequences when put into practice. These consequences, although foreseeable, were not in fact foreseen when divorce legislation was being enacted. The problem with legislation dealing with divorce is that, once a particular line has been adopted, it may be some years before its social effect can be estimated, by which time most errors may be irreversible.

Some obvious questions

Some obvious questions, therefore, arise. How has divorce actually worked out in other societies? Has divorce dealt effectively and humanely with the problem of unhappy marriages, or has it caused more problems and injustice than it has cured?

When examining the experience of other countries we must, of course, do so in a critical and sensible way. We must not assume that what happened abroad will necessarily happen here. We must have due regard to the fact that countries differ widely in their social and economic development and cultural norms. Moreover, we must constantly distinguish between problems associated with divorce and problems relating to marriage disruption. In the light of international experience, we shall try to examine whether modern divorce law necessarily involves certain social and legal implications for a society, having made the fullest allowance for social and cultural variations between countries. As the story unfolds, it will soon become clear that modern divorce law does indeed involve these implications.

One other point should be stressed at the outset. Our country is experiencing a significant problem of marriage instability; clearly this problem cannot be blamed on the existence of divorce legislation. The question we must answer is how best we can respond to the problem at a social and a personal level. This is no easy task: a social or legal policy may be very satisfactory for one married couple but extremely unsatisfactory and unjust for another couple. What works well for parents may result in hardship for their children. Personal interests, such as the pursuit of happiness and individual fulfilment, may tend to conflict with broader social and interpersonal responsibilities. The stark and basic question we must eventually face is whether the problem of marriage disruption will better be resolved by the introduction of divorce or by other social and legal responses. Clearly no solution is a panacea. Our responsibility is to make an informed decision, without emotion, in the light of the evidence.

Let us therefore examine the experience in other countries, asking a number of pertinent questions.

*   In cases of hardship does divorce law protect wives against being divorced?

*   Does the law ensure that(divorced)wives are adequately maintained?
*   How does divorce affect the succession rights of women? } Can
*   How would divorce affect the right to occupy the family [be
home now available to the wife and children? ‾ anaged
*   Does divorce law protect the interests of children? _yes_
*   Do reconciliation procedures really work under a divorce law?
*   Do court structures under a divorce law ensure that justice is done for the parties?
*   Does divorce weaken the stability of marriage?

Clearly, the answers to these questions should be found and studied before deciding whether the solution of divorce – which may seem in the abstract to be such a good one – is in fact the answer to the problem of marriage breakdown.

CHAPTER 2

The Modern Law of Divorce

When answering the important questions raised in Chapter 1 we must distinguish between two different systems of divorce. The first is the older system, generally known as *fault-based divorce;* this provides for divorce in cases of serious matrimonial misconduct, such as adultery or cruelty. The second system is generally referred to as *'no-fault' divorce,* or divorce based on 'breakdown of marriage'. Under no-fault divorce, where a marriage has irretrievably broken down, either spouse will be entitled to a divorce, without any consideration being given to the conduct of the parties. A point of some importance, which should be noted at the outset, is that under the no-fault system a divorce will be granted not only where both spouses wish it, but also in cases where *one* of the spouses does *not want to be divorced.*

The pressure for divorce nowadays is almost exclusively for no-fault divorce based on breakdown of marriage. No-fault divorce has been introduced in most countries in the relatively recent past and it has gained prominence only in the past ten years or so.

In this book, consideration will be given primarily to the proposition that a system of no-fault divorce based on breakdown of marriage should be introduced. This is the system that almost all proponents of divorce now favour. The philosophy of fault-based divorce appeals to very few people to-day. It is commonly accepted that, if a fault-based system of divorce were introduced in Ireland now, it would be supplemented or replaced by a no-fault system within a very short time. Nevertheless, since there may still be some proponents of fault-based divorce, consideration will also be given to the question of its introduction.

The term 'no-fault' divorce has not yet been used very often in this country and it might be thought that no-fault divorce is some esoteric system of divorce prevalent in some far off jurisdiction but of essentially no importance to the debate on divorce in Ireland. This would be a grave error. No-fault divorce based on breakdown of marriage has swept the world in little over ten years. From being a relative rarity only a decade ago in Western Europe and North America it has now become the norm. An examination of the divorce laws of most countries shows that this system of divorce has supplemented or replaced the former law almost everywhere. Where former fault-based grounds for divorce still exist they have remained in being (generally for reasons of political expediency) as a 'left-over' from a system of divorce which has been effectively rejected by the no-fault philosophy of breakdown of marriage. As the principles of no-fault divorce have become progressively clearer, the appendage of fault-based concepts of divorce has been removed in divorce systems of many countries.

Why has there been such a widespread move toward no-fault divorce? The reasons appear to have been complex. There was a desire to save couples from 'slagging matches' and scandal-mongering, and from the perjury and collusion which were identified as accompanying fault-based divorce. There was also a growing tendency to regard marriage breakdown as usually the result of incompatibility of temperament or of personality rather than the 'fault' of one spouse. Moreover, it was considered better that a dead marriage should be buried by divorce rather than have its empty shell preserved.

Nevertheless, the more thoughtful proponents of no-fault divorce realised that more was at stake than merely saving spouses from the bitterness of divorce proceedings. They appreciated that the philosophy of no-fault divorce has far more radical implications for spouses, children and society. The more careful advocates of the no-fault system could see that it implies a new structure of personal and economic relationships in society. These more fundamental implications have gradually become plain to a wide public through the build-up of experience of the operation of no-fault divorce during the 1970's.

The growth of divorce based on breakdown of marriage

Let us look at how no-fault divorce based on breakdown of marriage has become part of the law of most countries in recent times.

In England, no-fault divorce was introduced by the *Divorce Reform Act 1969,* which enabled a spouse to obtain a divorce against the wishes of the partner after five years' separation. The Act also provided for divorce after only two years' separation where both spouses consent to the divorce. In addition, the Act retained (with some changes) the former grounds of adultery, cruelty (now generally termed 'unreasonable behaviour') and desertion. A similar system of divorce was introduced in Scotland in 1976, and in Northern Ireland in 1978.

In Canada no-fault divorce was introduced by the *Divorce Act 1968.* The Act provided that a divorce could be granted after three years' separation where the divorce was consensual or five years' separation where the person seeking the divorce had deserted the other spouse. Several other grounds of both a 'fault' and a 'no-fault' nature (such as addiction to drugs, alcoholism, imprisonment, adultery and cruelty) were also included in the legislation. In 1976, the Law Reform Commission of Canada proposed that all these grounds for divorce should be replaced by the one ground of 'marriage breakdown', established in a formal judicial hearing by the evidence of one spouse, against which no opposing evidence would be effective. The Court would have no judicial function other than to record that a divorce had been decreed. This is increasingly becoming the legal model for a future development of no-fault divorce.

In the United States, no-fault divorce has swept the country over the past decade. California was a leader in 1969. Today, only Illinois and South Dakota have not introduced no-fault divorce grounds into their law. There has generally been a greater degree of frankness in the no-fault provisions introduced in the United States jurisdiction than in Britain or Canada: for example, there has been little pretence that under no-fault divorce law a divorce can be refused on the ground of hardship to the wife or the children. The periods of separation required before a divorce will be decreed tend to be short. Moreover, as early as 1969, before no-fault divorce had been widely tested in the United States, it was clear to leading proponents of no-fault divorce that, under this system, divorce may be granted without regard to any injustice this may cause the spouse or children of the party seeking a divorce.

In Western Europe there has been a rush to no-fault divorce in the past decade. In France legislation in 1975 introduced the right to obtain a divorce against the wishes of the other spouse after six years' separation; divorce by mutual consent and divorce based on a limited range of fault grounds, and divorce on the ground of incurable insanity are also permitted.

German divorce law has followed international trends. Legislation in 1976 made irreparable breakdown of the marriage the sole ground of divorce. Where the divorce is contested, breakdown is presumed where the spouses have lived apart for three years.

In the Netherlands, legislation in 1971 replaced the old fault grounds by a single ground of irretrievable breakdown of marriage. Divorce is now obtainable on demand by both spouses, or by one spouse against the wishes of the other.

In Italy, divorce has been obtainable since 1970. The grounds for divorce include a combination of fault and no-fault principles. But the most important ground, practically speaking, is the no-fault ground, which permits divorce after a separation varying from five to seven years, depending on whether the divorce is consensual or is sought by one spouse against the wishes of the other.

In Portugal, divorce based on contested grounds (such as adultery) and on mutual consent has existed since 1910. The practical effect of this law was, however, restricted by a concordat entered into by the Holy See and Portugal in 1940 whereby marriages contracted according to Catholic rites – nearly 90% of all marriages – were excluded from the scope of the divorce legislation. In 1975 the concordat was amended, making Catholic marriages susceptible to the civil divorce law. Two years later the grounds for divorce were extended: fault grounds have been retained but a divorce may also be obtained on the basis of six years' separation *de facto* or where the spouses have been separated by court order for two years.

In Spain legislation providing for no-fault divorce was enacted in 1981. A divorce may be obtained after a period of separation of one year (or in some cases two years) where both spouses consent to the divorce and after five years separation where one of the spouses does not wish to be divorced.

The Scandinavian countries have had a reputation in Europe for being more radical then elsewhere in the legislation affecting family relations. It is useful, therefore, to examine what has happened in those countries because some pointers for the future development of divorce law elsewhere may be obtained from such study.

Such an examination shows that whilst the divorce law in Scandinavia has perhaps been further relaxed than the divorce law of other countries in Europe and North America, it is clearly on the same road. The philosophy of no-fault divorce has been articulated more clearly in Scandinavia; consequently it is easier to see what fundamental implications no-fault divorce has for the family relationships in any society.

Swedish divorce law is contained in legislation enacted in 1973, following publication of a Report by the Committee on Reform of Family Law, in 1971. The values which were to control the Committee's deliberations had been clearly set out in 1969 by the Minister for Justice Herman Kling, when he appointed the Committee. Legislation, he said, 'should not under any circumstances force a person to continue to live under a marriage from which he wishes to free himself' and the new family law should 'so far as possible be neutral as regards different forms of cohabitation and different moral ideas.' Consistent with this philosophy, the 1973 *Marriage Code* provides that a spouse is entitled to a unilateral divorce as a matter of legal right; no reasons need be given; no 'breakdown' of marriage need be alleged, nor will the Court be interested in this question. The Court has no power to deny a divorce under any special circumstances, no matter how serious the implications of granting a divorce may be for the wife and children. The only protection that the wife and children have in such circumstances is a delay of between six months and a year before the divorce takes effect.

In Denmark, a divorce may be obtained by either spouse one year after a separation order or three years after *de facto* separation. There are also a number of fault-based grounds. Where both spouses wish to be divorced the divorce is obtained by an administrative procedure (usually lasting between ten and twenty minutes), without the intervention of any lawyer. In urgent cases, as for example, where one of the spouses is about to leave the country, a divorce based on fault may be obtained within one or two days of application.

In Norway divorce may be obtained after a period of legal separation: one year if the parties consent, but two years where the application is opposed. A divorce may be obtainable even in cases where it was the petitioner who broke up the marriage.

In Eastern Europe a system of no-fault divorce has prevailed for many years. (Indeed it has even been contended that the concept of no-fault divorce was born in the Soviet Union, but, as against this, it has also been suggested that Nazi Germany's divorce law of 1933 is the true source of no-fault divorce.)

In South Africa the *Divorce Act 1979* introduced radical changes, making irretrievable breakdown of the marriage as the only significant ground for divorce. The Court may accept as proof of irretrievable breakdown evidence that the spouses have not lived together as husband and wife for at least a year. In practical terms, divorce in South Africa is thus available after a year's separation, whether the divorce is sought by both spouses or by one spouse against the wishes of the other.

In Australia, divorce legislation in 1959 introduced no-fault grounds for divorce equivalent to those which were introduced in England ten years later: two years' separation was a ground for divorce where both spouses consented, five years where one spouse opposed the divorce. The 1959 legislation also included a large number of fault-based grounds. But the *Family Law Act 1975* adopted a far more radical approach. The no-fault philosophy has now completely obliterated the fault-based grounds. There is only one ground for divorce: 'that the marriage has broken down irretrievably.' The Court must grant a decree (whether or not one spouse objects) where the parties have lived separately for at least a year.

In New Zealand prior to 1980 a divorce might be ordered where the parties had been separated for at least two years and when the separation was not due to the wrongful act or conduct of the person seeking the divorce; it might also be awarded after four years' separation even where the separation was due to the wrongful behaviour of the person seeking the divorce. The *Family Proceedings Act 1980* has changed the position. Now, a marriage may be dissolved on the basis that the marriage 'has broken down irreconcilably' where the spouses have been living apart for two years whether by separation order, separation agreement or otherwise. The two year period applied in every case, even where one of the spouses does not wish to be divorced.

This brief review of the divorce law in other jurisdictions shows that no-fault divorce has swept the modern world over the past decade or so. Its basic philosophy is that a marriage should be terminated, not only where both spouses desire it but even where one spouse does not wish to be divorced. Although the legislation frequently speaks of the 'irretrievable breakdown of marriage', the blunt truth is that this is not a question investigated by the Court: the fact that one spouse seeks a divorce is in practice conclusively presumed to prove the existence of an irretrievable breakdown of the marriage. The only effective limitation on the right of one spouse to obtain a divorce against the wishes of the other is that of time: a delay of up to seven years' separation is required in some jurisdictions, although, as we have seen, far shorter periods of separation have been specified.

Future trends in divorce law

The universal trend in legislation is for the period of separation to be progressively shortened: once divorce based on breakdown of marriage is accepted, the pressure mounts inexorably for the period of separation to be reduced or removed entirely. It has been argued that there should be *no* period of separation since it could operate unfairly against women because it is usually easier for a husband to leave home than a wife. The same point has been made concerning the relative ease with which rich spouses may leave home as compared with poor spouses.

Another argument has frequently been pressed in favour of reducing or abolishing the requirement of a period of separation before a divorce will be decreed. It is said that such a requirement hinders the prospects of reconciliation between the spouses, since on separating they develop independent life-styles which militate against the prospect of reunion.

Another trend of some consequence is for divorce legislation to discard the old fault-based grounds, where these have been retained in the initial no-fault divorce legislation. Such fault-based grounds tended to have been included merely as a palliative to public opinion. They make no sense under a no-fault regime. Accordingly, when the no-fault principle has been part of the law for some years, the fault-based grounds are set aside.

A third and more radical trend is to regard the legal concept of marriage as redundant and to seek its abolition. The move to no-fault divorce has been perceived as an important element in the development of this trend. Thus, for example, Brenda Hoggett of the University of Manchester, having noted that family law in England 'no longer makes any attempt to buttress the stability of marriage . . . .', and having pointed to other changes in family law, argues that:

> Logically, we have already reached a point at which . . . . we should be considering whether the legal institution of marriage continues to serve any useful purpose.

All these trends forcefully confirm the statement of Professor Henry Finlay, a leading apologist for no-fault divorce, made nine years ago, when no-fault divorce was still a novelty in most countries:

> This then is the dilemma of our society. You either have to be restrictive or you can be permissive but you cannot be both at the same time. And having once started to be permissive, you are committed to being increasingly permissive. The process is a cumulative one.

CHAPTER 3

Divorce in Cases of Hardship

One of the crucial tests by which modern divorce law must be judged is whether it is a humane and just system. In particular, one may enquire as to what protection no-fault divorce affords to wives against being divorced in cases of hardship of a financial or other nature. If little or no protection is afforded, then (whatever other arguments may be put forward in favour of it) the *humanitarian* argument in favour of no-fault divorce is less compelling. One should at the outset distinguish between hardship caused by the disruption of the marriage, on the one hand, and hardship caused by the granting of a divorce, on the other. Clearly many women will suffer hardship from marriage disruption, whether or not a divorce is granted. But this does not mean that many women do not suffer further hardship from being divorced. One need only think of the damage to their rights of maintenance, succession and occupation of the family home, for example, to appreciate some of the potential areas of damage.

When no-fault divorce was being proposed in many other countries, its proponents claimed that under it protection could still be afforded to wives against being divorced in cases of hardship. Their assurances appeared to be supported by explicit provisions in the legislation introducing no-fault divorce.

Yet the experience, again and again, in countries which have introduced no-fault divorce is that *no substantial protection is afforded to wives against being divorced in cases where the divorce causes them hardship*. In England, Australia and Canada, the experience followed an identical pattern. The proponents of no-fault divorce legislation gave assurances that this protection would be afforded to wives. Provisions were included in the divorce legislation which appeared to do what had been promised. These provisions turned out to be quite useless in practice, with no protection in fact being afforded to these wives. This process was followed (sooner rather than later) by a realisation on the part of the judges that with no-fault divorce you cannot at the same time attempt to protect wives against being divorced in cases of hardship; the essence of the no-fault principle is that the desire of one or both of the spouses to terminate the marriage is to be the basis of entitlement to a divorce. Finally there has been an increasing tendency under no-fault divorce law to regard as a 'spoilsport' the wife who does not wish to be divorced in a case where the divorce will cause her hardship; as one Australian court put it, in such circumstances she should be regarded as a Shylock, seeking her 'pound of flesh.' Thus, within a very short period, it is promised protection of wives against the hardship of no-fault divorce has proved almost completely useless.

Whether it is desirable or undesirable that a divorce should be refused on the ground of hardship to a wife is, of course, debatable: even where the divorce is refused for this reason the wife (although in some cases financially better off) will still not have her husband back and the marriage relationship will be no more meaningful to the spouses merely because a divorce has been refused. But the international experience of the operation of the hardship defence is useful in showing that no-fault divorce does not and cannot effectively protect a wife against being divorced in cases of hardship. However politically attractive it may be to include a hardship defence in the divorce legislation, the fact remains that, when put into operation, it simply will not work effectively. Let us now briefly examine the experience of some countries on this question.

England

In England, when the *Divorce Reform Act 1969* was being enacted, the proponents of the legislation gave clear assurances that protection would be given to a wife which would extend not only to cases of financial hardship but to other cases as well. A decree for divorce would have to be refused where

> ' . . . . the dissolution of the marriage [would] result in grave financial or other hardship to the [respondent spouse] and . . . it would in all the circumstances be wrong to dissolve the marriage'.

Lord Stow Hill, who moved the Second Reading of the legislation in the House of Lords, proclaimed that 'the scales' could hardly be tilted more in [the wife's] favour.' This proved to be a false prediction: the provision has in fact afforded no substantial protection to wives. The reason is simple: the defence of economic hardship is inconsistent with the philosophy of divorce based on irretrievable breakdown of marriage. One or other has to give way. The defence of economic hardship therefore was sacrificed in the interests of free divorce.

What has happened in England is that the provision almost never has protected a spouse against a decree being awarded against her. Michael Freeman of London University, writing in 1978, seven years after the Act had come into effect, could trace only three cases in which a decree had been refused on the ground of financial hardship. Professor Dominic Lasok declared that the provision has 'proved to be largely decorative.' The approach of the Courts has borne out this description. As Ruth Deech of Oxford points out, they have 'recognised that such a defence has no justifiable place in the new law . . . .' The Courts have thus refused to protect women against the hardships of a divorce even though it has long been recognised that they are the primary casualties.

As regards the Court's obligation to refuse a decree where hardship of a non-financial nature is concerned, the position is still more distrubing. The Courts have consistently refused to listen to a plea that the granting of divorce will cause a wife to become a social outcast in her own community, such as the Hindu Community or Sicilian Society. Michael Freeman summarises the position:

'As a safeguard of religious and social susceptibilities the defence has proved, as was predicted seven years ago, ineffective.'

Writing in 1982, Stephen Cretney of the English Law Commission recorded that the defence of non-financial hardship has not been successful in any reported case.

Northern Ireland

Northern Ireland's divorce order of 1978, enacted by the Westminister Parliament, included hardship provisions similar to those in the English divorce legislation. During the parliamentary debates on the order Lord Simon, former President of the Divorce Division of the English High Court, stated that he had 'no doubt . . . . that this measure, like the 1969 Act, is utterly unjust to married women.' In no reported decision in Northern Ireland has the Court ever refused to grant a divorce against a plea of hardship. There is no reason to believe that wives in Northern Ireland will be afforded any more protection in practice than that contained in the English divorce legislation.

Scotland

The no-fault divorce legislation enacted in 1976 included a hardship clause, but limited only to grave financial hardship. The experience of the operation of the defence of financial hardship in Scotland suggests that no effective protection is afforded by it to wives.

Australia

When no-fault divorce was proposed in Australia, particular

concern was expressed by those who opposed the legislation about the position of abandoned wives. It was partly in order to counter these criticisms that certain safeguards were inserted in the divorce legislation of 1959. The most important of these safeguards were the requirements that a decree for divorce must be refused if by reason of the petitioner's conduct it would be harsh and oppressive to the respondent or contrary to the public interest to grant a decree and that a decree could not be made until satisfactory arrangements for maintenance had been made.

These protections in Australian divorce laws proved to be no more effective than their later English counterparts. Professor Finlay, writing in 1977, noted that 'the circumstances giving rise to their application were so infinitesimal in number as to be virtually non-existent.'

Mr Justice Selby describes the experience of the 'hardship' provision in Australia in frank terms. Referring to the legislation including these provisions he states:

> 'The pill is sweetened for the sensitive public palate by an attractive sugar coating . . . . Yet these are the very provisions which, to some extent, have proved unworkable, the safeguards which have been described as mainly illusory. The cynic might ask whether it was ever thought that these attractive provisions were workable or whether they were merely inserted as window-dressing to secure the passing of a Bill which might otherwise have had a rough passage.'

Not only did the courts fail to protect the wife against being divorced: they came to regard the wife, and not her husband, as being guilty of anti-social conduct if she placed any obstacle in the path of her husband in his desire to be divorced. In *Painter v Painter,* this attitude was expressed in forceful terms by the Court, which described spouses who resisted divorce on the grounds of hardship as insisting on their 'pound of flesh'. Australian law has now abandoned the fiction that, under no-fault divorce, a decree can be refused on the ground of hardship. Legislation enacted in 1975 makes no provision for such a possibility.

Canada

The same tale unfolds in Canada. Provisions were included in the Federal *Divorce Act* of 1968 designed to protect women against divorce in cases of hardship, but these have proved ineffective.

In Canada one finds the same hostility as was apparent in

Australia towards wives who seek to invoke these provisions. Thus, for example, the Law Reform Commission of Canada in its Working Paper on Divorce uses language that displays less of the judicial detachment than perhaps one might have expected from such a body:

'Under present divorce procedures, a spouse may give vent to his or her vindictive desires by filing a defence to divorce and using or, more accurately, abusing available procedures and practices to harass the other spouse or delay a final judicial disposition.'

The courts take the same view; Dr Hahlo of McGill University states that it is not unusual, in cases where the respondent intends to fight the divorce, for the presiding judge

'instead of praising the respondent's devotion to the institution of marriage, [to] do his best to persuade the parties and their counsel to conclude an honourable divorce settlement, rather than battle to the last ditch.'

The attempts by Canadian women to oppose a divorce on the grounds of non-financial hardship have been no more successful in Canada than in England or Australia. Writing in 1975, seven years after the *Divorce Act* had been enacted, Dr Hahlo reported that he knew of *no* case in which a woman had been successful.

Europe
No-fault divorce legislation in Europe is generally of more recent origin than that in the English-speaking countries. In some countries, an effort has been made to protect wives by including a 'hardship' clause, but in others the reality of no-fault divorce has been admitted and no hardship clause has been included in the legislation.

In Western Germany, divorce legislation enacted in 1976 enabled a spouse to obtain a divorce against the wishes of the other no matter how serious the hardship which the granting of a divorce would involve for the other spouse. (The draft legislation had contained a defence based on hardship but this had been struck out by the parlimentary law committee as being incompatible with the concept of breakdown.) The only brake on granting a divorce in such a case was that the spouse seeking the divorce would have to wait five years: but once five years had elapsed, the divorce had to be granted no matter what damage was caused thereby to the other spouse.

In France, a divorce will be refused if it entails 'material or moral consequences of exceptional hardship' for a spouse, taking account of his or her age, and of the duration of the marriage, or for the children. In some cases the courts appear to have gone further than their English counterparts in refusing to grant a divorce, but in doing so have provoked criticism on the basis that they acted contrary to the philosophy of no-fault divorce. Moreover, there is a risk of 'forum shopping' by husbands seeking to divorce their wives in cases where hardship may result for the wives: these husbands may seek to have the divorce proceedings heard by a judge who would not regard the 'hardship' defence with sympathy. Since the *Cour de Cassation* (the French Supreme Court) accepts as correct the findings of fact of any judgment that is appealed, the wives in such a case may be in a vulnerable position.

As has already been mentioned, the divorce legislation in Sweden enables a spouse to obtain a divorce as a matter of legal right, without stating reasons or alleging any breakdown of marriage, whether or not the other spouse wishes to be divorced. The Court has no power to deny a divorce, no matter how serious the implications of granting a divorce may be for the other spouse and children. All they can ask for is a delay of between six months and a year before the divorce decree takes effect.

The lesson for Ireland

The international evidence on this question has an important lesson for Ireland. The experience in other countries clearly indicates that the law cannot confer on a husband the right to divorce his wife against her wishes without at the same time denying to her protection against being divorced in cases of hardship. All commentators now accept this, and, as we have seen, the thrust of legislation is now towards increasing frankness and the removal of provisions which originally appeared to provide protection, but failed to give it.

As Dr Holden commented (after a review of the hardship provisions in England, Australia, New Zealand and Canada), such bars 'run counter to the breakdown principle on which divorce following separation is based.' And, as Deech and Eekelaar have observed, the defence of hardship 'runs counter to the notion of divorce without fault . . . .'

CHAPTER 4

Financial Support after Divorce

How does modern divorce law affect the right of wives to be maintained by their husbands? Surely this is a central question which should be resolved before contemplating the introduction of divorce into out law. At present, married women have substantial rights to maintenance from their husbands, backed by a variety of enforcement procedures, including attachment of earnings. The effect of divorce would be to reduce these rights, and in some cases to abolish them entirely.

The experience of countries which have introduced divorce based on breakdown of marriage is that men are released from their former level of obligation to maintain their wives. Men have been arguing – with considerable success – that the philosophy of modern divorce requires that dead marriages should be buried and that, if the marriage is dead, so also should their obligation to maintain their wives come to an end. The men have said to their legislators: 'In allowing divorce on demand you gave us a licence to remarry with no questions asked. In order to make that right to remarry effective rather than merely theoretical, you have to cut us off from a continuing responsibility to maintain our first wife.' Neither the legislators nor the courts can resist the logic of this argument, so they have bowed to it and have severely reduced and in some instances abolished the first wife's right to be maintained after the divorce.

But where does this leave the wife, especially in cases where she devoted her life to rearing children within the home and has not continued in a career outside the home? The experience in countries which have adopted no-fault divorce is that the wife frequently is consigned to social welfare assistance at subsistence level.

She is told that divorce and marriage breakdown inevitably cause financial hardship and that for this reason she must suffer in silence. To add insult to injury, the very introduction of divorce based on breakdown of marriage is itself invoked as a basis for denying continuing maintenance to wives. The argument – again an entirely logical one – runs as follows: where marriage is a permanent institution from which neither spouse can walk away at will it is reasonable that it should involve continuing obligations of maintenance; but with divorce based on breakdown of marriage, marriage is clearly no longer a permanent institution; therefore it is not fair to impose a continuing obligation on a husband to maintain his wife after the relationship has ended, for whatever reason. As the English commentator, J.D. Green graphically put it, for the law to permit no-fault divorce *without* reducing the husband's maintenance obligations to his divorced wife would be

> like giving a toy to a child, and then taking it away from him the moment he begins to play with it. He will be uncomprehending, for why give it to him unless he is meant to play with it? The ex-husband will be no less uncomprehending. Why allow him to re-marry, knowing that he cannot afford to support two families, and then impose such financial burdens on him that in all probability his second marriage will go the way of the first, and that even if it does not, it will be reduced to penury?

It is probably fair to say that these alarming consequences, although inherent in the philosophy of divorce based on breakdown of marriage, were not generally appreciated by most people when this system of divorce was being introduced in their countries. But today the issue is clearly one to which we should give detailed analysis. In chapter 12 we will discuss some of the more important issues; in the present chapter we will examine in detail the international experience regarding maintenance of wives under modern divorce law.

England

When the *Divorce Reform Act 1969* was being enacted, the proponents of the legislation claimed that the divorced wife's financial interests would be protected by just and effective legal provisions. Certainly the legislation sounded encouraging: it required the courts, in making an order for the maintenance of the wife and children, so to exercise their power

> as to place the parties, so far as it is practicable and, having regard to their conduct, just to do so, in the financial position in which they would have been if the marriage had not broken down and each had properly discharged his or her financial obligations and responsibilities towards the other.

The reality has proved to be nothing like what this provision would suggest. In 1980 the English Law Commission, in its Discussion Paper on the financial consequences of divorce, referred to this statutory provision as having served 'little useful purpose', being 'constantly nullified in practice' by the qualification that the court should only act 'so far as it is practicable.'

Writing in 1980, Mary Hayes, of the University of Sheffield describes the position more bluntly:

> Usually it is the first wife and children who are left unsupported .
> . . .

Moreover, as the English Law Commission explains, divorced wives are frequently driven (on account of lack of adequate support from their husbands) to resort to supplementary benefit from the State 'at a subsistence level.'

The Commission reports that many divorced wives:

> resent their dependence on what seems to them to be an inadequate level of State support and the drop in their living standards following the breakdown of the marriage, and this is particularly so where their husbands have remarried, and seem able to enjoy a high standard of living.

Finally, where a divorced wife seeks variation of a maintenance order to take account of the reduced value of money over the period since the order was granted on divorce, she may be in for a rude shock. The English Law Commission states that

> It seems that in practice, even in times of high inflation, an application for variation is more likely to result in a decrease rather than an increase in the sum ordered to be paid.

In spite of this position of divorced women being awarded inadequate maintenance, the general pressure in political and judicial circles in England is to reduce the woman's rights to maintenance still further. As has been mentioned, men have been complaining that they do not like having to continue to support their divorced wives, and they argue that, if the marriage is dead so also should their obligation of maintenance come to an end. These men have been joined by some feminists who regard marriage and maintenance as part of an economic structure which reinforces the dependency and exploitation of women.

The men's argument has been heeded by the law reform agencies. In December 1981, the English Law Commission published a Report entitled *The Financial Consequences of Divorce*. The Commission now recommend that the Court in divorce proceedings should no longer seek to place the spouses in the financial position in which they would have been had the marriage not broken down. Furthermore they recommend that

> The importance of each party doing everything possible to become self-sufficient should be formulated in terms of a positive principle; and weight should be given to the view that, in appropriate cases, periodical financial provision should be primarily concerned to secure a smooth transition from the status of marriage to the status of independence.

The Commission also consider it desirable to require the Court specifically to consider whether an order for a limited period of time would not be appropriate in all the circumstances of the case, given the increased weight which, according to the Commission's proposals, would be attached to the desirability of the parties becoming self-sufficient.

The Commission present a very summary analysis of the intended effects of their proposals in relation to the maintenance of divorced women. It is clear, however, that the principal intended effect is to reduce the already inadequate levels of maintenance still further. Let us look for a moment at the Commission's proposal that each spouse do 'everything possible to become self-sufficient, so far as this is consistent with the interests of children.' If it means what it says – and why should it not? – it would have serious implications for some divorced wives, especially older wives whose children have grown up. Let us take as an example a woman aged fifty-five who is divorced by her husband. Her four children have now grown up and are married. In her youth the woman worked as a bookeeper; she still has an excellent head for figures. According to an employment consultant produced as a witness in the divorce proceedings by her husband, she is still employable. Under the Commission's proposals this woman must do 'everything possible to become self-sufficient', so she must either contemplate returning to employment or face the prospect of reduced maintenance from her husband.

Early this year the government announced that it would introduce legislation to give effect to the English Law Commission's proposals.

Scotland
In November 1981, the Scottish Law Commission published its *Report on Aliment and Financial Provision*. The Commis-

sion recommended that 'the principle of fair provision for adjustment is independence' after the divorce requires that *the dependent spouse (almost invariably the wife) should receive financial provision for a period of not more than three years from the date of the divorce to enable her 'to adjust . . . . to the cessation of that dependence'*.

The Commission consider that in certain limited circumstances an extension beyond three years would be justified. These would involve cases of hardship that arose from the marriage, as where a wife contracted a disabling disease in a tropical country where she had gone with her husband, or where a wife became prematurely disabled as a result of injury in childbirth. But the Commission stated that they had

> More doubt about whether a former spouse should ever be expected to relieve the hardship of the other if the hardship does not arise in any way from the marriage. If we were approaching the matter as one of pure principle we would be inclined to reject such a proposition as contrary to the idea that divorce ends the marriage.

Nevertheless, because it recognised that it was essential that any system of financial provision on divorce should be acceptable to public opinion, the Commission proposed that an extension should be permissible in a case where *at the time of the divorce* it seemed to the Court that a spouse would suffer *grave* financial hardship. Two points may be noted regarding this recommendation. First, the expression 'grave financial hardship' (as we have seen) is part of Scottish existing divorce law in that a divorce based on five years' non-cohabitation may be refused where the grant of the decree would result in 'grave financial hardship' to the spouse who does not wish to be divorced. In almost no case has a divorce been refused in practice on this ground. If the expression 'grave financial hardship' is to be interpreted in the same way in relation to maintenance after divorce – and the Commission would appear to accept that this may be so – then it seems reasonable to predict that in few cases will maintenance be awarded for a period of longer than three years after the divorce.

The second point is that the Commission make it abundantly plain that they consider that an extension beyond three years should never be made, no matter how severe the financial hardship suffered by the spouse, save in cases where the *likelihood of hardship* was established at the time of the divorce. Thus, for example, where a woman was paralysed as a result of a road accident or where a progressive disease was diagnosed shortly after the divorce, no extension beyond the three-year limitation period for maintenance would be permitted. After that period, each spouse 'should be free to make a new life without liability for future misfortunes which may befall the other.'

The Commission's recommendations are made against an economic background of hardship and lack of effective employment opportunities for married women in Scotland. The Commission itself acknowledges that there is

> abundant evidence that, although married women are increasingly in paid employment outside the home, and although the policy of the law is firmly against discrimination on grounds of sex or marriage, it remains the case that women, and married women in particular, have not as a general rule gained anything like complete equality in the employment market. Their employment is often part-time and their earnings are low.

Canada

The position of divorced women in Canada is little different from that in England. Professor Hahlo has identified the move to no-fault divorce as involving a reduction in the wife's ability to safeguard her economic position relative to that of her husband's. He states that

> Once the guilt principle is jettisoned, an economically dependent wife is deprived of her bargaining power . . . .

The future looks equally bleak for divorced women in Canada. The Law Reform Commission of Canada in its *Report on Family Law* has proposed that the entitlement of divorced women to maintenance should be reduced still further.

United States of America

The same story unfolds in the United States of America. Writing in 1979, of the experience there, Bianca Larson stated that

> Contrary to a woman's expectation of fair treatment . . . spousal support for the majority of women remains at best a myth or at worst a cruel joke.

The same point is made by Professor Krause of the University of Illinois. He states that the move to no-fault divorce in the United States has generally

> made divorce less burdensome for the economically stronger and more burdensome for the weaker partner.

Similarly, Sachs and Wilson report that

> 'No-fault' divorce is not a perfect solution by any means because in practice there is some evidence indicating that it reduces the amount of support allocated to needy women since technically no one is at fault. This is obviously a sexist implementation of what was intended to be a progressive, sex-neutral reform.

Joel Holt has predicted that the future trends will be further along these lines:

> the wife will have a harder time getting a decree of support, and when she does, the amount will be smaller.

Professor Joan Krauskopf, of the University of Missouri-Columbia, who is an expert in alimony and matrimonial property, explains that

> Those involved in the legislative process creating 'no-fault' divorce were aware that it would create a new hazard to the economically dependent wife. Under the former system most divorces were ultimately non-contested but the result of negotiation in which the wife, who ordinarily did not wish to be divorced if she needed the economic security of marriage, would halt his attempts to divorce her. With the demise of . . . the recrimination grounds that same woman would be dangerously vulnerable.

What has happened in the United States (as elsewhere) is that, with the introduction of no-fault divorce, the economic security of wives has been sacrificed *without* the necessary social and economic equality having been attained. Bianca Larson describes the position:

> In actuality, the job market for women is dismal. The fact remains that women will face a job market geared to the married male. Despite the rapid growth of the female labour force in re-

cent years, a woman seeking employment will find only a limited number of jobs available. The United States Supreme Court recognised that continued economic discrimination against women and the socialization process of a male dominated culture combine to make 'the job market . . . inhospitable to the woman seeking any but the lowest paid jobs'.

Women are primarily concentrated in low paying female-intensive industries and occupations. Unfortunately, little headway has been made in sex-desegregating highly paid, male-intensive fields, such as management, the trades, and certain professions. Moreover, contrary to public opinion, the disparity between women's and men's earnings has actually increased.

Comparable educational attainment does not decrease this disparity, nor do women fare better in high paying job categories such as the professions or skilled technician positions. Women who have devoted their lives to homemaking often lack the experience and recognized skills necessary to compete in the job market. Single women with young children face the additional problem of inadequate childcare, which makes employment an impossibility for many. As long as women continue to face special problems in the job market, their need for spousal support will remain.

A number of empirical studies have been carried out in the United States on the effects of no-fault divorce on the economic position of wives and children. These studies reveal a consistent picture of severe economic distress.

Professor Thomas Espanshade of Florida State University reports the findings of surveys in the United States on the subject of the economic consequences of divorce. He states that in general wives are left worse off than their former husbands. Not only are they usually the ones awarded custody of the children without sufficient financial help from fathers, but they generally face other impediments in the labour market regarding higher pay and adequate employment opportunities.

A separate study was carried out recently by Professors Lenore Weitzman and Ruth Dixon of the University of California into the effects of no-fault divorce on alimony awards to women. It reveals some important findings. First, the study showed that, under no-fault divorce, awards to wives in marriage of less than five years' duration were virtually eliminated. In Los Angeles County, the percentage of wives awarded permanent alimony dropped from 62% in 1968 (before the introduction of no-fault divorce) to 32% in 1972 (after the introduction of no-fault divorce). The drop in San Francisco County during the same period was from 57% to 42%. One of the most important findings of the study is that, contrary to the expectations of the researchers, it revealed that *the rate of awards of alimony to mothers of pre-school children declined more rapidly after the introduction of no-fault divorce than for any other category of children.*

Perhaps the most disturbing facts revealed by the report concerned alimony awards for older wives who were clearly not self-sufficient at the time of the divorce on account of having pursued the career of housewife rather than a career outside the home. Professors Weitzman and Dixon note that the proponents of no-fault divorce argued that the effect of no-fault divorce would be that these women would be guaranteed alimony because of their impaired earning capacity. But this is not at all how it has turned out. Their study reveals that only in cases where the ex-husband has a substantial income will such wives be assured of getting any alimony at all. If he does have substantial income, she has about a 50/50 chance of alimony – despite the standards and ideals of the no-fault divorce law.

Similar findings were made in a study published in 1979 by Dr Karen Seal of Grossmount College. Dr Seal found that, under no-fault divorce, maintenance was awarded less frequently to divorced wives; when maintenance was awarded the amount tended to be smaller; and less child support was awarded.

> Mothers of minor children in the study were also financially harmed by the introduction of no-fault divorce legislation. In almost all cases, they were awarded custody but were not given the same financial resources as mothers divorced under the [former] system. The children in the no-fault cases tended to be younger and to be supported by their fathers for a shorter period of time. In addition, the wife was ordered to pay a share of the family's debts while the family home and other assets were usually divided.

Dr Seal explains that under the former system of divorce the home and furniture usually went to the wife, 'allowing her to maintain a semblance of home life while raising the children.' But under no-fault divorce the amount of child support awarded was less than formerly, so there was no financial compensation for the loss of assets and the assumption of liabilities by the wife.

A study of divorced spouses and their children was conducted over a period of five years by Judith Wallerstein, of the University of California, Berkeley, and Joan Berlin Kelly, Director of

Children's Services in the Community Mental Health Centre of Marin County, California. Five years after divorce, the position was as follows:

> Half the men continued to be solidly upper and upper-middle class. With few exceptions the women were poorer than they had been during their marriage and appeared likely to remain so. One-third of the women were emmeshed in a daily struggle for financial survival. The absence of adequate support seemed particularly disturbing in families whose economic situation before separation had been reasonably secure.

The future

Almost everyone in countries with even fault-based divorce is aware of the phenomenon of the hardship of divorced wives who have devoted their lives to their families. But the philosophy of no-fault divorce requires that the law be changed still further so as to give less rather than more protection to divorced women. As an Australian commentator, C.M. Butler, points out 'it is elementary that revolutionary changes in the law of divorce must be accompanied by corresponding alterations in the law of maintenance . . . ' Dr Kevin Gray of the University of Cambridge articulates this philosophy very clearly:

> The decree of divorce will effectively operate as a licence to remarry, by returning the erstwhile spouses to single status in the eyes of the law and thereby enabling them to avoid the criminal sanction attaching to bigamy. The law of reallocation of property must be similarly directed towards reinstating the spouses as single persons in economic terms, by replicating insofar as possible the financial portion which each would have enjoyed had the marriage never taken place. In other words, the law must attempt to restore to each the financial independence which he or she had before marriage, and thereby terminate the economic relationship of marriage with the same degree of finality which attends the conclusion of the spouses' personal relationship. Any attempt artifically to preserve the parties' respective financial position as if the marriage had not broken down is premised as a profoundly misleading fiction which, in the context of serial marriage, becomes quite ludicrous. Divorce must mean what it says – a complete termination of the marriage relationship. Accordingly, the resolution of economic matters on divorce must aim at effecting, in the truest sense, a *restitutio in integrum*.

In simple terms what is being proposed here is that, after

divorce, a husband should be treated by the law as a stranger towards his wife: strangers do not owe each other continuing obligations of support; therefore, the husband should not owe his wife an obligation of support.

But does this not mean that many wives will in many cases be reduced to subsistence level after divorce – especially wives who have opted to rear children in the home? Unfortunately it may indeed, say the proponents of no-fault divorce. So, what solution would they offer to this problem? Their answer is that if the divorce legislation makes it absolutely clear to wives that they will not be adequately supported after divorce, the legislation, as Dr Gray points out, will then

> mould expectations and influence work patterns during marriage until eventually the need for post- [divorce] support very largely disappears.

What is being predicted here is that, on marrying, women will realise that they cannot expect to receive adequate support from their husband if the marriage ends in divorce. Therefore, it is argued, they will, in their own economic self-interest, seek to protect themselves by staying in full-time employment during marriage.

Of course, in Ireland and abroad, women in increasing numbers are remaining in full-time employment after marriage or returning to full-time employment some years afterwards. Far from being forced into employment, many of these women (though scarcely all of of them) find true fulfilment in their work. But just as this is so, it is equally the case that many thousands of women in Ireland work in the home. We have seen that an intended effect of introducing a system of divorce based on breakdown of marriage would appear to be that every woman should take up employment outside the home.

This brings us to a more general, but important, issue which has been lurking in the background of our discussion of divorce. Proponents of divorce have frequently sought to invoke the changing concepts of sex roles in society today as a justification for the economic hardship which no-fault divorce involves for women. Women who seek the legal entitlements which were their due until no-fault divorce was introduced are told that they ought not complain because in society today women should cease to be dependent on men and should stand on their own feet: since divorce emphatically obliges them to attempt to do this, it should, the argument runs, be regarded as being in the interest of women in the long term. Such a view has the support of many (though not all) feminists and is consistent with the more general perception of marriage as an institution which enslaves women, or which at least restricts their opportunities for economic and personal autonomy.

This perception of marriage is scarcely dominant in contemporary Irish society, although it seems reasonable to assume that it is gaining increasing support as time goes by. Indeed the position may well be reached at some future date when this radical analysis of marriage actually does represent the view of Irish society. But that day surely has not yet arrived. What more probably is the view of most people here today is that women should be given full opportunities to work outside the home and that in some cases (especially where there are no children and the wife is young) it may not be appropriate for wives to look to their husbands for support. But most people (including many wives) probably also consider that it would be far from every case where this would be so. It seems fair to assume that there is a reasonably broad range of opinion on the role of women in today's society. Whatever may be one's opinion about the *desirability* of the views which the majority of the community hold on sexual equality, it is important to be aware that these views are still current, and are not likely to change overnight. *The particular problem with divorce in the Irish context is that many women would be bound to suffer economic hardship from its introduction, with no guarantee that other radical changes in sex roles, which might mitigate this hardship, will take place in the immediately foreseeable future.* It would be naive to believe that those who would today support the introduction of divorce on broadly humanitarian grounds are committed on that account to a radical change in sex roles. Yet, if divorce is introduced without this radical change, women will suffer substantial economic hardship, as is already the experience of women in many countries which have adopted no-fault divorce. This issue will be examined in more detail in chapter 12.

Support obligations during a marriage
Let us examine a little closer a further implication that flows

from the view that, on divorce, the spouses should be regarded by the law as strangers to each other with no continuing obligations of support. A predictable consequence of removing the obligation of maintenance *after* divorce is that the pressure will mount, over a period of time, for the removal of the obligation *during the currency of the marriage.* It would be very difficult in logic to defend the imposition of a maintenance obligation on a spouse during marriage only for as long as the spouse wishes to be under the obligation. Indeed, a legal system which insisted on imposing such an ineffective obligation would rightly be regarded as adopting an inconsistent and futile approach. It could be argued that if the law imposes maintenance obligations on a spouse during the marriage but relieves him of these obligations on divorce, this would have the effect of encouraging him to terminate the marriage in cases of disharmony so as to obtain a legal release from the obligation to maintain his wife. *A logical implication, therefore, of the introduction of a system of divorce based on breakdown of marriage would be for the law to remove the obligation to maintain one's spouse during the currency of the marriage. Such a development would worsen still further the economic plight of married women. It would undo many advantages for women that were brought about by the recent maintenance legislation in Ireland, in 1976.*

This complete reversal of present legal policy deserves closer examination. The position of women whose husbands have deserted them or failed to maintain them was the subject of particular concern in the country in the early 1970s. Michael Viney's penetrating study, published in the *Irish Times* in 1970, led the way. Several women's organisations (notably AIM), and the Commission on the Status of Women sought changes in the law so as to impose effective obligations of maintenance on defaulting spouses. The *Family Law (Maintenance of Spouses and Children) Act 1976* brought about radical improvements, by creating a right to apply to the Court for a maintenance order where a spouse fails to provide proper maintenance for the family. The Act also introduced a system of attachment of earnings to supplement the somewhat cumbersome (and arguably ineffective) sanction of imprisonment for defaulting in payment.

The policy to which the Act gave effect was warmly welcomed by leading members of women's groups, including Nuala Fennell – the only criticism being that the policy should have been even more stringently enforced. Senator Mary Robinson, for example, welcomed the Bill and commended the Minister for Justice for 'the thoughtful and enlightened way in which its provisions are framed.' She described the Bill as 'a very good solid piece of family law reform within its limits', and she regarded section 10, which related to attachment of earnings, as 'a very welcome and very desirable provision. This has been sought for a long time by women's groups, such as AIM, and other groups. It is a very important provision.' Referring to the experience in other countries (including Britain), as to the effectiveness of attachment of earnings, she stated: 'therefore I think it is important to ensure that the procedure is as watertight as we can make it.' As we have seen, the policy of the Act runs completely counter to the philosophy of divorce based on breakdown of marriage. The Act seeks to protect the maintenance rights of women as effectively as possible, whereas no-fault divorce seeks to release the divorced husband from his full responsibility to maintain his first wife.

The lesson for Ireland

The evidence from countries which have adopted no-fault divorce shows that the inevitable pressure is for the maintenance rights of divorced women to be limited and in some cases abolished. Moreover, this development makes it difficult to defend the imposition of spousal maintenance obligations during the currency of marriage. The effect of these changes is that many women who work in the home are likely to be the primary casualties of divorce, as they are in other countries. Attempts have been made to defend divorce on the basis that it is consistent with the principles of women's liberation, but experience in most countries shows that changes in divorce have been introduced without the changes necessary to protect women against hardship. The result is that many divorced women get the worst of both worlds. Unless there is a commitment by society when introducing no-fault divorce to bring about the same time a radical and all-embracing change in sex roles many women will be the inevitable casualties. The question of divorce has tended to be perceived as raising issues of humanitarian and pluralist concern rather than as involving a radical transformation of sex roles. It is scarcely likely that if divorce were to be introduced in the near future in this country, such transformation in sex roles would on that account also be made. International experience (even in countries where feminism has a far broader appeal) suggests strongly that this would not be the case. It is more likely that the change would be a slow and gradual one. If this is so, many women must suffer, as they are at present in other countries, without the prospect of relief in the foreseeable future.

CHAPTER 5

The Succession Rights of Women

The effects of divorce on the law of succession would be significant. The losers would be divorced women.

Under existing law a married woman has substantial succession rights. Where the husband dies without having made a will
and there are no children the wife is entitled to all of his property; if there are children she is entitled to two-thirds and the
children share the remaining one-third of his property. Where
the husband has made a will then the wife has a legal right to a
half of his property if there are no children and a third of the
property if there are children. These legal rights will override
any attempt by the husband to disinherit his wife by leaving his
property to some other person.

An important right attaching to the wife concerns the family
home. The *Succession Act* of 1965 seeks to protect the wife's
right to occupy the home after her husband's death, by permitting her to appropriate the home in full or partial satisfaction of
her succession rights. Moreover, where the Court is of the opinion that in the special circumstances of the case hardship would
otherwise be caused to the wife and children, it may order that
the appropriation of the home is to be made without payment of
money, even though the value of the home exceeds the value of
the total entitlements of the wife and of any children for whom
she is a trustee. These rights are very substantial and
cumulatively they afford a wife very considerable protection, especially in cases where her husband may not have had her best
interests at heart.

*How would women fare as regards succession rights under divorce? All
the evidence from other countries show that they would fare badly. The
general tendency is to reduce the succession rights of divorced women, and in
some cases to abolish them completely.* Thus, in New Zealand and
New South Wales, for example, a divorced wife has no rights under the Testator's Family Maintenance legislation. As Judge
Davern Wright observed:

> 'Although destitute and innocent of wrongdoing, she has no right
> to apply under the Acts.'

Similarly in Ireland, if no-fault divorce were introduced and the
legislation followed the example of other countries, a wife whose
husband had deserted her would lose some or all of her existing

rights of succession to his estate.

Under divorce law, the *second* (or subsequent) wife rather than the first wife has first claim to the man's property when he dies. Most men die in middle-age or older. If a middle-aged man divorces his middle-aged wife in order to marry a younger woman, the younger woman rather than the former wife will be entitled to most of his property when he dies. Perhaps some may defend this result on the basis that a woman who has been divorced has less moral claim than a new wife. Others may consider it unfair that the former wife should have her succession rights reduced in favour of the younger woman. However one feels about the result, the important fact to note is that *if divorce is introduced into our law, the present succession rights of married women will be reduced, as they have been in other countries, in favour of the new wife.*

It is true that in those counties where the divorce law includes provisions for equal distribution of property on divorce, some of the detrimental effects on succession would be mitigated since the wife would be entitled to a share of her husband's property at the time of divorce rather than when he died. But it would be wrong to conclude that, in conferring this right on the wife, divorce is some way gives a benefit to a wife which she could not have if there were no divorce. Greater benefits would accrue to her if the law conferred on both spouses equal rights to matrimonial property as an inherent element of the marriage relationship from the first day of the marriage. This reform will be discussed later.

CHAPTER 6

Divorce and the Family Home

Until fairly recently wives and children in Ireland had relatively limited legal protection against the home being sold over their heads by the husband. There were reports of wives first discovering that the home had been sold when they answered the door to the new owners. Women's groups were universal in their condemnation of this position. The Commission on the Status of Women in its Report in 1972 recommended that the law be changed so as to protect women against this scandal. This was done when the *Family Home Protection Act 1976* was enacted. The Act gives wives very substantial protection against the vindictive sale or mortgage of the home by their husband. It requires the prior consent of the wife for the sale or mortgage of the home made by the husband. Her consent can be dispensed with only where, on application to it, the Court holds that the wife's refusal is unreasonable. Further substantial protection is afforded to wives by a provision which makes it a crime for a husband (or other person) to attempt to defeat the policy of the Act; moreover, the wife has a right to substantial damages against her husband if he disposes of the home without her consent.

The legislation was strongly supported by politicians and women's groups, the only complaint being that it did not go further by giving women a property right in the home. Senator Mary Robinson, for example, described the Bill as 'very useful and important.' She noted that

> Probably the source of greatest hardship in our family law has been the helplessness and the dependence of the wife who could not prevent the matrimonial home from being sold over her head. She could not protect herself and her children from this hardship and she was solely at the mercy of whatever goodwill her husband would show her when the marriage relationship had broken down. If he wished to desert her and sell the home and realised his asset there, she could not prevent it.

The Bill was, she said, an 'extremely significant' measure, which would have a deep psychological and cultural impact in the country. Senator Robinson referred to a Report on separation agreements which had been recently published by the AIM group. That report had referred to the fact that the separated wife could not prevent the matrimonial home from being sold over her head. Senator Robinson commented: 'That is one of the matters that will be remedied by this Bill.'

How would wives and children in Ireland fare under no-fault divorce? Would they still be protected against being evicted from the home? Or, instead, applying the philosophy of no-fault divorce, would they lose their right to occupy the home?

The experience of other countries is that after divorce is introduced security in the home can no longer be guaranteed by the law. In England, for example, the (somewhat limited) statutory protection for wives against being evicted from the home generally ceases to operate on divorce. Of course in many instances the court granting a divorce will (under other statutory provisions) exercise its discretion in favour of the wife's continued occupation of the home but this is not always the case. Moreover, the practice in England of ordering the home to be sold when the children have reached the age of eighteen (or in some cases, younger) means that a divorced wife may be evicted from the home in late middle-age, — a result which some commentators find regrettable. The experience in the United States should also be noted. It was reported in 1979 by Drs Bumpass and Rindfuss that under the divorce law there

> In addition to associated status loss, substantial alterations may be required in life style, perhaps the most significant of which is the frequent inability of the mother to retain the previous home. Moving under these circumstances is itself a strain, compounded by the fact that the move may often be to a poorer neighbourhood.

Dr Seal's study, published in the same year, reported similar findings. It showed that, before the introduction of no-fault divorce based on breakdown of marriage, wives in California were granted the home and the furniture, but that, after no-fault divorce had become part of the law,

> The home . . . . must be equally divided so the couple sells it and splits the proceeds, or the wife pays the husband his equity, or she relinquishes some other comparable asset such as her interest in his pension plan. Selling the home causes dislocation of the wife and children and loss of any leverage that she might have had to insure his payment of support.

The study describes this development as 'one of the cruelest byproducts of no-fault divorce' in California. It states that property values have escalated to such an extent that purchasing another home is 'virtually impossible for all but a small minority of working women' who have been divorced.

One should not, of course, understate the serious economic consequences that may in some cases result from marriage breakdown irrespective of any question of divorce: there simply may not be enough money to ensure that the wife and children will be able to remain in the family home. Whether or not there is divorce, the courts frequently will have considerable practical difficulty in ensuring that adequate protection can be given to the interests of all parties. But divorce tends to make the position worse rather than better. As we have seen, divorce based on breakdown of marriage involves the principle that if the marriage relationship is dead the spouses should be treated as strangers. This principle has now been openly accepted in respect of the continuing obligation of a man to maintain his wife after divorce. The same principle implies that the wife should not have a continuing right to occupy the home. For why should a divorced man be required to keep a woman who is now a stranger in continuing occupation of what was the family home? If she has no claim to maintenance in the form of cash from him why should her claim to bricks and mortar be any more effective? If she is to fend for herself in earning her living after a divorce why should she not also have to find and pay for her own accommodation? Why should she be a drain on her husband's resources in this respect any more than in respect of maintenance?

In England the Campaign for Justice in Divorce expresses in unusually frank terms the philosophy and policy of no-fault divorce towards protecting the wife and children's occupation of the family home. The Campaign criticises the courts on the basis that they

> place an exaggerated and unfair emphasis on the needs of children when decisions are made on the disposal of assets, particularly the matrimonial home and contents . . .

The Campaign argues that moving house

> 'is part and parcel of normal family life and no one regards it as unacceptable. Yet when there's a divorce suddenly all these normal events are regarded by the court as something to be avoided. This is the main reason why the courts so often endeavour to keep the mother and children in the matrimonial home regardless of the hardship this inflicts upon the father, who usually is deprived

of all his capital. The bitterness and resentment this common decision causes is frequently visited upon the children and the father's ability to maintain his relationship with them is prejudiced or prevented because he has less chance than the mother of providing suitable accommodation. This is against the interest of the children as well as being grossly unfair to the father. He is expected to collect them from the comfortable home, which in all probability he provided in the first place, and take them back to his tiny flat or bed-sit.'

Whether or not one agrees with this analysis, the philosophy on which the Campaign proceeds comes through clearly: if divorce is to be granted on the basis that no responsibility attaches to the husband, why should he have to keep his wife and children in the home? The logic is unanswerable.

CHAPTER 7

Children's Rights under No-Fault Divorce

Introduction

How have children fared under divorce? Have their rights to maintenance been protected by the law? Do the courts guarantee that their interests will be protected? Or are children ignored by the law of divorce?

The evidence from countries with a modern system of divorce is that the interests of children have been largely ignored. Moreover, the effect of placing an increased obligation on a divorced mother to support her children at the same time as reducing the mother's economic resources by denying her adequate maintenance from her husband, has naturally been that less money is available for the children, who in most cases will be living with their mother rather than with their father.

The future seems to hold no immediate prospect for improvement: indeed, there are some indications that the position of children will get still worse. The logic of the no-fault divorce philosophy appears to be gradually working its way through to children, as it already has done in relation to spouses. The argument is again a simple one of impelling logical force. It runs as follows: No-fault divorce regards divorce and marriage breakdown as the responsibility of no one: they are akin to a death in the family. If no one is responsible, then it is unfair to impose on the children's father, who is just as much a 'casualty' as the children, the obligation to maintain them after the divorce to the extent formerly required before the introduction of no-fault divorce. Men are also arguing that, if they have little or no contact with their children after divorce, they should not be required to support them.

These developments are so alarming – yet so completely consistent with the philosophy of no-fault divorce – that they must provoke considerable caution in responding to the argument that no-fault divorce protects the interests of children.

Let us examine in detail the experience in other countries relating to children under modern divorce law.

England

When the *Divorce Reform Act 1969* was being enacted the proponents of the legislation gave assurances that the interests of children would be protected in divorce proceedings. A divorce decree would not be granted, it was promised, unless the Court was satisfied that the arrangements made for the children were satisfactory or the best that could be devised in the circumstances. Moreover, in considering whether to grant a decree based on five years' separation, the Court would have to consider the interests of the children.

Experience has shown that, in over nine cases out of ten, the Courts do not even adjourn proceedings for further information regarding the child's welfare where the parents are agreed as to the custody of the children. Moreover, it seems that no greater interest is shown by the solicitors of the parties, who must draw up the documentary evidence for the Court, setting out the proposed arrangements for the children. A recent survey carried out by Mervyn Murch in Bristol has shown that 80% of solicitors never even met the children in question.

John Eekelaar of Oxford stated in 1976 that the following description by Hansen of experience elsewhere 'probably aptly describes the situation prevailing today in England and Wales':

> The pious 'concern for the welfare of the children' becomes a thin cloak for a massive indifference to the impact of the divorce decree upon the future lives of the children.

Dr Alec Samuels of the University of Southampton has noted that the pressure on social workers is so great that in many cases the social inquiry report regarding the children is 'positively discouraged.' He states: 'in effect there is little restraint upon the parents pursuing their divorce aspirations'. According to Dr Samuels, the English law relating to the protection of children in divorce proceedings 'presents an unpleasing aspect. The jurisdiction is fragmented. Children are "ancillary" to parents'.

Before concluding that the English approach is clearly deficient, we should perhaps enter a *caveat*. Some commentators, while accepting that divorce courts perform a very limited supervisory and protective function in relation to children, argue that this may not be so bad for children as might at first appear. These commentators generally subscribe to one or both of two schools of thought. The first school of thought has much support in the United States; it takes the view that parental autonomy and privacy in decision-making should prevail over the intervention of the State (whether through judicial or administrative agencies) : in summary, that there should be a presumption that parents rather than the State know best what is good for their children. The second school of thought is less ambitious: it goes no further than arguing somewhat fatalistically that judicial supervision is unlikely to achieve very much, especially where the parents are united on a course of action relative to their children which the court may regard as not being in the children's welfare.

Let us now examine the position of maintenance of children after divorce in England. In a Report published in April 1981, entitled *Maintenance: Putting Children First,* the National Council for One Parent Families paints a most distressing picture. The Council notes that dependent children are involved in over 60% of divorces. It states that 'there are strong indications that very little maintenance is paid to the vast majority of one-parent families that are the consequence of divorce and separation.' The Council also notes that over 61% of one-parent families headed by women are dependent on State benefits as their main source of income. Furthermore, it records that in around 32% of one-parent families the single parent goes out to work even though she has children to care for.

In a telling passage in its Report, the Council states:

> The principle that, in making decisions about the upbringing of a child, the court must regard the welfare of the child as a first and paramount consideration has never been expressly applied to the question of *maintenance* as opposed to custody or access. Moreover, it is quite clear that the courts do *not* put the children's interests first when deciding property and ordering maintenance on divorce.

The Council concludes its analysis of the present position by stating that: 'Far from being the first consideration, the maintenance of the children appears to be the last consideration in actual practice.'

In similar vein Jennifer Levin of London University stated in 1981 that it 'is certainly not the position in actual practice' that the law on maintenance for children in England is governed by the principle that the welfare of the child is the first and paramount consideration. She stated of divorce proceedings that:

orders for children; indeed it is doubtful if they ever have much information before them on what it really costs to keep a child. Basic issues, such as how far in assessing a child's maintenance the cost of looking after the child, as opposed to feeding and clothing him, etc., should be taken into account, are uncertain. It is likely that in the majority of cases the maintenance paid to wife and child together will not in fact be enough to keep the child.

The English Law Commission in its Report, *The Financial Consequences of Divorce,* published in 1981, appears to accept that Jennifer Levin's description of the position is correct. It proposes that the legislation should clearly embody the principle that the interests of the children should be seen as a matter of overriding importance. But the possible benefits of this proposal are largely subverted by the Commission's limitation that 'such a provision cannot increase the amount of money available for the custodial parent and child'. In other words, the present position described by Levin of maintenance awarded to wife and child together not being enough to keep the child will not be improved.

United States of America

The position of children under divorce law in the United States is far from satisfactory. The number of divorces involving children has increased alarmingly in recent years, yet, as Professors Sabilas and Ayers state,

> Often the interest of children is the least considered area in 'the American way of divorce '.

So also Professor Paul Conway, of Georgetown University, has noted that

> the most unfortunate effect of divorce, and the greatest social problem it generates, arises from its debilitating effect upon children.

Professor Michael Wheeler has perceptively noted that

> Ironically it is concern for the welfare of children that often sparks interest in improving our family laws, yet, after the dust of reform has settled relatively little has been done for them.

Developing this theme Professor Foster and Dr Freed report that no-fault divorce 'has enhanced the risk that the welfare of children may be downgraded or overlooked'.

The empirical studies that have been published bear out these statements. A detailed empirical study of the making and enforcement of child support orders was carried out in Denver by Professor Marsh Lee of the University of Denver in 1978. The study found that 'children of men who, in fact, have enough money to support them are being supported by other taxpayers.' A separate study carried out by Dr Seal in California revealed that under no-fault divorce child support awards slipped from a median amount of 900 dollars to 732 dollars per annum. Similar findings were recorded in a study by Weitzman and Dixon.

As in other countries, empirical evidence indicates that it would be simplistic to attempt to explain the inadequate levels of support for children in the basis simply of the father's inability to pay. Data from the General Accounting Office in 1974 indicated that there is 'little relationship between a father's ability to pay and either the amount of the payment agreed to or his compliance with the law.'

Canada

The experience of children in Canada is little different to that in other countries. As Mr Justice Wright stated in the Ontario decision of *Bray v Bray:*

> I should point out what I believe most Judges sitting in divorce in Canada would allow to be true, namely, that in many independent cases the children of the marriage are the victims or pawns of their parents' urges to divorce or to remarry and that much of the evidence and attitude and agreements as to custody which attend divorce proceedings are to secure the divorce and not necessarily to protect the children.

The level of child support in Canada is disturbingly low. The Manitoba Law Reform Commission has expressed the view that 'sometimes payment of child support is assessed and awarded at unrealistically low amounts.' The Commission had received information from persons who complained that in some areas in Manitoba child maintenance was being fixed by the Court (in 1976) as low as twenty five dollars a month - that is, about £4 a week.

A pilot study of active cases in the British Columbia Provincial Court at Vancouver yielded an average rate for awards between 1976 and 1978 of approximately 71 dollars per month – that is, about £11per week – per child. But even this modest sum was inflated by a minority of large awards. Moreover, it had apparently remained constant in the seventies and had not kept pace with rises in the general wage structure or the cost of living.

The authors of a paper sponsored by the Canadian Ministry of the Solicitor General and the Ministry of the Attorney-General for British Columbia expressed the view that the reported mean size of child support awards made on divorce

is so meagre as to arouse suspicion that the focus is much more on the needs of the [father] than on his obligations.

This view is supported by the findings of a study by the Canadian Institute for Research in relation to the economic plight of divorced women in Canada.The study published in March 1981 showed that lack of sufficient income to meet their obligations was *not* the reason for failure by many men to maintain their divorced wives and children. The results of the study suggested that the ability to pay depended on the priority accorded to maintenance payments relative to other financial obligations. Thus, the failure by the men to provide support for divorced wives and their children was attributed in part to

continued feelings of belligerency towards their ex-wives, dissatisfaction over custody and access arrangements, and feelings that they had been treated badly by the legal system.

Australia
Detailed provision for the protection of children, very similar to those in the subsequent English legislation, were introduced into the Australian divorce legislation of 1959, but to no avail. Neville Turner, describing the effect of the provisions, noted that 'regrettably, it is doubtful whether the interests of the children are safeguarded in practice by any of these measures.' Section 71 of the Act provided that a decree of divorce was not to be made absolute unless the Court had, by order, declared that it was satisfied that 'proper arrangements in all the circumstances have been made for the welfare of [the] children', or that there were special circumstances by reason of which the decree should become absolute notwithstanding that the Court was not satisfied that proper arrangements had been made. Commenting on these provisions, Mr Justice Burbury stated that he found it

very difficult to escape the conclusion that in most cases the protection intended to be given by the Act to the children is largely illusory.

These provisions were included in somewhat expanded form in the legislation of 1975. There is little reason to believe that this change has afforded significantly greater practical protection for the interests of children.

The future

The future prospects for children under modern divorce laws are not bright. Already there is pressure for a further reduction in the divorced father's obligations to his children. In England, the Campaign for Justice in Divorce has made proposals along these lines. We have seen earlier that the Campaign contends that

> The courts place an exaggerated and unfair emphasis on the needs of the children when decisions are made on the disposal of assets, particularly the matrimonial home and contents, and the amount of child maintenance.

We also noted its argument that it is improper for courts to attempt to ensure that children can continue to live in the family home after divorce. In its view, moving home for children 'is part and parcel of family life.'

The Campaign recommends that maintenance of a child should terminate in all cases at the age of eighteen (even though the child might be mentally or physically disabled). It considers it 'wrong to continue child maintenance' beyond this age. Further, no maintenance should be paid when the child leaves school, for whatever reason.

The recommendations of the Campaign for Justice in Divorce may seem to some people to be unjust. On reflection, however, the proposals, if one can ignore their inhumane aspect, have some logic. At least they are consistent with the perception of divorce as involving the reduction of economic responsibilities towards the first family which, as we have seen, is the logical conclusion of divorce based on irretrievable breakdown of marriage. Moreover, if justice and personal responsibility are to be regarded as irrelevant to the relations between husband and wife, there may be a tendency to place less stress than formerly on their relevance to relations between parent and child.

Of course it is easy to see a distinction between spousal and parental obligations: spouses who are not maintained can (in some cases at least) seek employment, but children, especially young children, have no such option. Moreover, spouses entered into their relationship with each other voluntarily, but the child clearly had no say in being born. For this reason in countries with divorce the prevailing view may in the future be that it is reasonable to deny a wife the right to be maintained by her husband while at the same time imposing a continuing obligation on parents to maintain their children. But it would be unwise to ignore the danger of the development of the no-fault philosophy so as to weaken, and ultimately destroy, the obligation of parents to maintain their children. As we have seen in relation to England, there is already evidence that this trend has begun in some quarters, although so far strongly resisted by the English Law Commission. We would do well to monitor the position there: we can surely learn from the experience of English children under a modern divorce law in coming years.

Lessons for Ireland

The experience of children under divorce in foreign countries surely has a number of lessons for Ireland although these must not be exaggerated. Our own procedures in relation to children where a marriage breaks down are unsatisfactory in a number of respects. Nevertheless two points emerge from the international evidence, which we will discuss in chapter 12. The first is that divorce has proved no panacea for children. Contrary to what was prophesied by proponents of liberal divorce, courts granting divorces have paid only little attention to the interests of children. The second is that the philosophy of no-fault divorce has alarming implications in relation to the child's maintenance: if the father is to be regarded as a 'casualty' of marriage breakdown, like his child, why should one casualty be called on to support another?

If divorce were introduced into our law, would the same results follow here? The short answer must be that they would not necessarily do so. The international experience in relation to the custody and maintenance of children has not the same *necessary* implications for this country as does the international experience in relation to such a matter as the maintenance of spouses, for example, where definite and unambiguous implications in relation to the operation of no-fault divorce in this country can be discerned. But it is surely only prudent to recognise that, if no country with divorce has come up with satisfactory solutions in relation to children, the onus of proof must rest on those who claim that an Irish divorce law would be

CHAPTER 8

Separation and Children: the psychological effects

It is sometimes argued that divorce is desirable because a child will be happier where his parents are divorced than where the family remains together in continuing matrimonial discord. One preliminary objection to the argument is that it equates separation with divorce. Whilst separation may well be desirable in certain instances of disharmony, it does not follow that divorce is also desirable. The economic damage which women and children suffer from divorce is in itself a good reason for distinguishing between separation and divorce in this context.

There is another objection to the argument that children are happier where the family splits up than where the spouses remain together in matrimonial discord. The argument wrongly assumes that, under a modern divorce system, only spouses who have been in continuing matrimonial discord will be divorced. As we will see in Chapter 11, experience has shown that divorces are sought (and granted) in some cases where there has been no history of continuing matrimonial turmoil.

The argument therefore does not succeed in showing that *divorce* is desirable, but it certainly raises some interesting separate questions on which it is sensible to have information. What is the effect of the divorce process on children? How do children adjust to the double trauma of separation and divorce? Does a divorce, by changing the status of the parents, ease the unhappiness and emotional disturbance which children suffer, or do the problems remain or get worse?

Dr Futterman, Clinical Professor of Psychiatry and Pediatrics at the Child Study Centre of Yale University, has stated that 'recent studies have challenged the earlier belief among professionals that divorce is better for children than unhappy marriages, and the deleterious effects of post divorce turbulence have been well documented.' The most comprehensive research has been carried out in California by Wallerstein & Kelly, culminating in a book entitled *Surviving the Breakup*, published in 1980. The study examined in depth the effects of divorce on sixty families over a period of five years, concentrating on the experience of the children. The study's findings are of course limited by its selective criteria and by the race and class of its subjects : we should bear these factors in mind when addressing its significance. In a detailed discussion of Wallerstein and Kelly's book, Michael Freeman, Reader in English Law at University College London, states

> 'The book is unquestionably the most illuminating documentary evidence of the divorce process yet published . . . . If it's a truism that divorce does not end the problems of marriage, the evidence for it is in this book in abundance . . . . If there is a more important book on the divorce process published in England then I have missed it. *Surviving the Breakup* has all the signs of being a classic in its field.'

As Michael Freeman notes

> 'Wallerstein and Kelly demonstrate that children actually prefer an unhappy marriage to their parents' divorce.'

As far as the pre-adolescent children are concerned,

> 'divorce was a bolt of lightning that struck them when they had not even been aware of the existence of a storm.'

Wallerstein and Kelly found that, at the time the parents separate, the child is

> 'intensely worried about what is going to happen to him. Whatever its shortcomings, the family is perceived by the child at this time as having provided the support and protection he needs. The divorce signifies the collapse of that structure, and he feels alone and very frightened.'

Wallerstein and Kelly found that there was an important link between a child's success in coping with the divorce and his capacity to understand and appreciate the significance of the sequence of disruptive events in the family. But they also found that in two out of three divorces no such rational foundation existed. In cases where divorce had been sought by an emotionally disturbed parent, Wallerstein and Kelly found that

> 'The children in these families and the marital partner who opposed the decision [to divorce] were often bewildered and distraught. And moreover, . . . since the decision to divorce did not address any particular problems in the marriage, there was no subsequent relief or sense of closure.'

There were also impulsive divorces, which were 'undertaken without reflection or planning or any real consideration of the consequences', as, for example, where a divorce petition was used as a strategy to punish an adulterous partner or to induce reconciliation.

The authors analyse the response of the child to divorce in a section of the book which has been described by Michael Freeman of London University as involving 'both skill and insight'. They demonstrate that divorce is a frightening experience:

> Children and adolescents alike experienced a heightened sense of their own vulnerability. Their assurance of continued nurturance and protection, which had been implicit in an intact family, had been breached. They confronted a world which suddenly appeared to have become less reliable, less predictable, and less likely in their view to provide for their needs and expectations. Their fears were myriad. Some were realisitic; others were not. The specific content of the worry varied with age and child and family, but the anxiety itself was a widespread phenomenon, and appeared as a central response.

They describe the acute depressive symptoms, sleeplessness, restlessness and difficulty in concentration, feelings of emptiness, play inhibition and various somatic complaints suffered by children of divorced parents.

Divorce is also a time of worry for the child, often about the father, who is in most cases the non-custodial parent. Wallerstein and Kelly state:

> The departure of the father from the household is an extraordinary event. Especially for the younger ones the departure was terrifying . . . .

Moreover, more than half the children worried intensely about their mothers. 'They were aware of a new feeling of precariousness, of being dependent on one rather than both parents together.'

Divorce is also a time when the child feels rejected. Wallerstein and Kelly report that

> The children experienced a parent's departure from the home as indicative of a diminished interest in them. The parents' preoccupation with their own problems and partial withdrawal of in-

terest in them, and the interruption in their care seemed a further rejection. Young children particularly were unable to understand one parent's departure from the other as different from leaving them. As a result, over half the children suffered intensely from feelings of rejection by one or both parents during this critical time.

Wallerstein and Kelly report that the loneliness of the child at this time is 'profound . . . . acute, painful, and long remembered . . . .' They state that 'The loneliness which most youngsters experienced was frequently wedded to the sense of rejection and to the yearning for the intact family or the departed parent.'

A painful conflict of loyalties also arises. The children of the divorced family

> feel pulled by love and loyalty in both directions. Often the conflict is exacerbated by parents and, indeed, two-thirds of the parents openly competed for the children's love and allegiance. Even when this did not occur, the child had a sense of divided loyalties. Schoolage children particularly appeared to conceptualize the divorce as a struggle in which each participant demanded one's primary loyalty, and this conception greatly increased the conflict and unhappiness of the child. For, by its logic, a step in the direction of one parent was experienced by the child (and sometimes by the angry parent as well) as a betrayal of the other, a move likely to evoke anger and further rejection. Some children refrained bravely from stepping in either direction, out of a sense of honour and love of both parents. They faced, instead, the consequences of aloneness, with a despairing sense of having no place to turn for comforting or parenting. Their conflict of loyalty placed them in a solitary position midway in the marital struggle. For most children this was a new position, one which they had not even been pressed to take during the conflicted marriage.

Wallerstein and Kelly report that children and adolescents of all ages experienced a rise in aggression. Temper tantrums increased in the youngest children, as did the hitting of other children and siblings. A quarter of the children 'experienced an explosive anger' which they directed at both parents. Beyond this, for over a third of the children, especially but not exclusively among the older boys, anger was a major accompaniment of the separation experience. While some of the aggressive behaviour was, doubtless, stimulated by witnessing parental fighting, the authors report that beyond this, the children considered the divorce an act of selfishness in which the parents had given primary consideration to their own needs and only secondary consideration to the children.

Wallerstein and Kelly's study establishes that the response and behaviour of children to divorce differs according to their age. The youngest children, in the group of those under six years of age, becomes regressed and feel bewildered and betrayed:

> Sometimes the fear of being hurt or betrayed in a relationship spreads to the relationship with the teacher in school.

The youngest children may see themselves as replaceable, in just the same way as they perceive their fathers to have been. They are unable to make the sophisticated conceptual distinction between their father's departure being directed at their mother rather than at them.

Wallerstein and Kelly report that for children under the age of six

> The routine separations of daily life were suddenly filled with dread. Some clung to the remaining parent, whimpering or crying when the parent left on a routine errand or departed for work at the usual time, or went out for an evening. Parents who returned from work or retrieved their children after school were greeted with angry tears, crankiness, and sometimes tantrums by children sufficiently relieved by the parent's return to express the anguish and frustration which they had suffered during the parental absence. Anxieties arose as darkness approached, and peaked at bedtime, which soon became a tense and unhappy battle of wills between an exhausted angry parent and a panic-stricken child. Throughout the night children became fretful, waking frequently, crying and begging to be taken into the parent's bed.

Children of this young age elaborated fantasies in response to the departure of their father:

> One fairly common fantasy which children expressed in their play was their fear of being left hungry by their parents. This fear of hunger was associated with their fear of abandonment and with the consequences of aggression.

Wish-fulfilling fantasies were also intensively employed, especially by the little girls, to help them cope with their painful sense of rejection and loss:

> The children's loyalty and intensive love for the father remained unchanged, despite repeated disappointments in the post-separation relationship. Several of these little girls remained nourished for many years by vivid fantasies about the father and his expected return. These fantasies clearly served to reverse the unbearable sense of rejection, of not having been loved sufficiently, if at all.

Another finding in relation to these children was that

> One immediate impact of the divorce can be considered a disruption in the pleasure of play. The youngest children, particularly, experienced play inhibition and appeared burdened and constricted as they constructed unsafe toy worlds populated by hungry, assaultive animals.

Children in the age group from six to eight years experienced somewhat different responses to their parents' divorce. The authors report that for this group of children

> the most striking response . . . . was their pervasive sadness. The impact of the separation appeared to be so strong that the children's usual defenses and coping strategies did not hold sufficiently under the stress. Crying and sobbing were not uncommon, especially among the boys . . . Unlike the preschool children who made extensive use of fantasy to deny the separation and loss and who held fast to the idea that someday their family would be reunited, these children, more intensely conscious of their sorrow than any other group in the study, had great difficulty in obtaining relief. Sometimes the intensity of the child's distress was directly related to the amount of turmoil generated between the parents, but some children suffered acutely where there was no overt or apparent parental upset.

Like the younger children, children from six to eight years were also frightened by the collapse of their family and had many unrealistic fantasies, including the fear of being left without a family or of being sent to live with strangers. Fantasies of being deprived of food and of toys also pervaded the thinking of many children.

The study found that the yearning of the children in this age group for their father was particularly striking, the intensity of the response bearing no relation to the degree of closeness between the father and child during marriage. The authors attempt to explain this finding on the basis that

> inner psychological needs of great power and intensity were being expressed. Separation from the father, at this crucial age, may threaten to disrupt the process of   identification with the father.. Moreover, the threat of regression may be particularly frightening for these children, especially for the little boys who have newly resolved oedipal conflicts and who now experience the anxiety of being alone with the mother, without the father's reassuring and constraining presence.

Children in the age group from nine to twelve years had a still clearer response to divorce. The unhappiness that they experienced often galvanised them into vigorous activity which was

> a composite of coping and defensive strategies designed to help overcome those feelings of powerlessness which the children in this age group experienced as so humiliating and so threatening to their equilibrium.

Some of these children tried to bring about a reconciliation between their parents. In others, the researchers found that there was

> a fully conscious, intense anger . . . well-organised and clearly object-directed . . . . Their capacity to articulate their anger directly was striking.

Some children in this age group experienced a shaken sense of identity. Part of this confusion related to their sense of right and wrong and to their conscience which is very much in formation at this time of life. The study found that

> Children felt that their conscience had been weakened by their disenchantment with the parents' behaviour, and with the departure of the very parent who had more often than not acted as their moral authority.

Finally, the study found that children in this age group were particularly vulnerable to being swept up into the anger of one parent against the other: there was a tendency to align with one parent - usually the mother - against the father.

For adolescents the problems were somewhat different. Again anger and a profound sense of loss were common responses. Loyalty conflicts were also apparent. The study found that

Other family functions crucial to maintaining adolescent development were also weakened by the divorce. These included providing discipline, external structure, and controls. The shaky family structure of the newly divorced family and the loosened discipline of the transition period combined with parental self-absorption or distress to diminish the available controls. Some of the youngsters lacked inner controls, the consolidated conscience and independent capacity to make judgements that they needed to maintain themselves without strong parental support and guidance. The divorce left them feeling vulnerable to their own newly strengthened sexual and aggressive impulses, and surrounded by the temptations of the adolescent world without the supports that would hold them to a straight course. Although many youngsters were able to maintain their own course, their efforts to do so were costly.

The study also found that many adolescents were 'terribly vulnerable' to the fear that their parents' divorce foreshadowed their own future failure in love and marriage. Specifically the normal anxiety levels about sexual performance 'were increased many fold.'

Adolescents expressed 'a profound sense of loss'. They reported feelings of emptiness, tearfulness, difficulty in concentrating and chronic fatigue, which the authors of the study identified as symptoms of mourning. Again, anger was a common response, the children considering that their parents had given priority to their own needs. The study found that many adolescents 'attempted thoughtfully to learn from their parents' failures to become better, more mature adults . . .', moving more quickly into psychological independence and maturity. But the study also found that many other adolescents responded to the greater pressure 'by hanging back and turning towards childhood or toward a pseudoadolescent adjustment.'

This important study thus indicates that children of all ages can suffer when their parents' marriage relationship collapses. The recurring picture of children suffering guilt, fear, loneliness and anger (documented in several other independent studies) should remind us of the very important effects of parental conduct on children. To ignore this dimension, and to concentrate exclusively on the parents' relationship with each other, may result in unintended but serious damage to children on a large scale. Of course, the type of damage documented by Wallerstein and Kelly was not created by divorce (save in certain cases where the availability of divorce led to the termination of what was a viable marriage relationship): the real source of the problem was the disruption of the marriage. But the study is important in affording evidence which puts into proper perspective the simplistic and over-broad assertion that, from the standpoint of children, divorce is the solution for unhappy marriages.

English experience

It is interesting to note the experience in England. In Spring 1982 John Eekelaar of the University of Oxford published the results of a research project conducted at the centre of Socio-Legal Studies, Wolfson College, Oxford. The project sought its data from cases referred to divorce court welfare officers for a report. Welfare reports were more likely to be sought in cases where the number of children involved was large; where a child had moved between parents after separation and before the divorce petition; where it was proposed that the child's residence should be changed; where it was proposed non-relatives (other than a cohabitee) were in the household; where the children were split between households; and where the children were living with persons other than a parent. The children studied were thus belonging to a pre-selected group, the selection being made 'on the basis of a perception that the[se] cases contain elements indicative that the family breakdown contains higher risks of hardship or disruption to the children than "normal" cases.' This perception is a commonsense, but provisional one, since there is as yet no conclusive evidence as to the extent of relative levels of hardship and disruption in these two groups of children.

Eekelaar reports that 'one of the more disturbing findings of the research' was that in 31.9% of the cases the welfare officer recorded signs of emotional disturbance in one or more of the children. As their main source of information, the officers drew on reports from schools recording aggressive or attention-seeking behaviour, but they also reported what parents told them and, of course, what they observed. In ten of the thirty-nine cases where emotional disturbance was found, reference was made to the involvement of specialist outside help, such as Child Guidance Clinics, educational psychologists, psychiatrists and medical practitioners. In only one case was delinquency expressly mentioned. Eekelaar counsels that

> In considering what weight is to be put on the officers' recording of emotional disturbance, it should be remembered that the officers are members of the probation service, well accustomed to dealing with deviant young people. Their threshold for recording

'disturbance' is thus likely to be higher than that of people who are less familiar with aberrant behaviour.

The friendly divorce

In recent years much thought has been given to developing procedures which will reduce conflict between divorcing parents, and protect their children from emotional damage. Already in the United States some parents have gone to great lengths to make their divorce a friendly, co-operative one, without acrimony or struggles over custody, support and access. Experience suggests that their attempts to save their children from damage may be less than fully successful. Dr Edward Futterman of Yale University's Child Study Centre reports that

> Children from such apparently benign marriage dissolutions may come to the attention of the child psychiatrist long after the actual divorce with such problems as aggressive acting-out behaviour, declining academic performance, poor socialization, depression, [and] diffuse anxiety . . . .

Many of the problems documented by Wallerstein and Kelly may also manifest themselves in these friendly divorces: Dr Futterman records feelings of rejection, anger, anxiety and heightened loyalty conflicts. He states that

> Reunion and reconciliation fantasies are particularly stimulated by these 'friendly' divorces. Even a remarriage might not dissuade the youngster from holding on to the wish that his parents get back together again.

Of course the lesson to be learned from this study is not that parents should be discouraged from co-operating with each other after they have separated. Obviously, any mitigation of the damage that children suffer is to be welcomed. The value of this study lies in showing just how difficult it is for divorcing or separating parents to shield their children from the harmful emotional consequences.

Relationship between step-parent and child

Let us now turn very briefly to an important aspect of the debate about the effects of divorce on children which so far has received far too little attention. This concerns the relationship between children and *step-parents* after a divorce. Although the subject has not yet been comprehensively studied by the experts nevertheless, as Professor Judith Younger of Cornell University noted in 1981, 'even before their results are in, there are signs that the reconstituted family is a poor environment for the young'. She states that

> The adults in reconstituted families are fighting legal battles to secure rights of access to the children, and to determine what their names should be and who shall adopt them. The resulting tensions are bound to disturb the children, who have their own problems, and to affect the stability of their families.

According to another American commentator (Norman), these families

> are often beset with jealousies and conflicts of loyalty not found in traditional families. Sometimes, children who resent the experience of divorce either cannot adapt to the new family or try to tear it apart. And many husbands and wives carry into their second marriage the attitudes and behaviour that ruptured their first.

Similarly, Justice Elizabeth Evatt, Mr Justice Watson and Mr Don McKenzie, reviewing Australian experience, state that children who are involved in successive relationships

> suffer considerable impact because of impermanence . . . . The child may have difficulty in identifying with a 'new' parent and, at the same time, maintaining a relationship with an 'old' or intermediate parent. The 'old' or former parent may feel displaced, and the 'new' parent uncertain as to his or her role. Consequently problems arise. For example, should the child's surname be changed to that of the 'new' family? How far should the 'old' parent insist on visitation, thereby disrupting the routine of the 'new' family? Relationships in the 'new' or 'reconstituted' family are frequently under great stress, where the old parent is not dead, but divorced.

In a sensitive account of English experience, published in 1981, Martin Wilkinson explains that the responses of parents to the new partner may have effects on the children. He states:

> The emotional responses of both parents and children to this event will vary enormously according to individual circumstances, but it is safe to predict that few of them will be wholly positive . . . .

If the second partner has been directly involved in the events leading up to the marriage breakdown, the disapproval will be obvious and specific in its manifestations. It will be expressed with the most vehemence when the second partner was known to both parties before the liason began; this is as sure a recipe as any for access problems. Even when he or she is newly come upon the scene and was not involved prior to the marriage breakdown, the fact of being replaced and of therefore being finally cast off must always be to a greater or lesser extent unpalatable.

It is rare indeed for these negative feelings not to be transmitted at least in part to the children of the family. The potential, so far as access is concerned, will inevitably be for ill rather than for good.

Experience in Canada, reported by Drs Messinger, Walker and Freeman of the University of Toronto, identifies sexual tension as another complicating factor that may arise in the relationship between children and their step-parent. There is also evidence that frequently children feel threatened by the decision of their parent to bring a new partner into the family group, leading to the unfortunate dilemma for the parent as to whether to remarry if the child says it would make him or her unhappy. The authors report that the issue of remarriage confronted many of the participants in their study as

> a choice between the right of the adult and the needs of the child. The consensus . . . . was that parents do have the right to remarry, but that they must recognize the pain experienced by children who have to accept and live with their parent's decision to bring a new parent figure into the family. The members were in general agreement that if parents allowed the child to break up a relationship, it would damage the parent-child relationship and place a heavy burden of guilt on the child.

A most discouraging description of the difficulties involved in relationships between children and their step-parent is given by Dr Emily Visher, Vice-President of the Stepfamily Foundation of California, and Dr John Visher. They report that

> While there are jealousies and the intensity within nuclear families varies, the intensity of these feelings is greatly magnified in step families.

Stepmothers in families where the father has custody of his children tend to make great efforts to live up to the expectations of these children but, in attempting to do so, 'many stepmothers neglect their own children . . . . This pattern often leads to subsequent guilt and resentment, particularly in families in which the stepchildren do not respond positively to the stepmother's overtures.'

The same study states that one of the hardest problems that many fathers face is dealing with their guilt about leaving the children of their previous family and becoming the stepfather of a new family:

> Sometimes the feelings of guilt are so strong that the stepfather is unable to enjoy his stepchildren. He cannot give freely and openly to the stepchildren with whom he lives, because of his guilt at depriving his natural children of fatherly affection and concern. In extreme cases, the stepfather may develop strong resentments and antagonisms towards his stepchildren, and there may be a complete inhibition of warmth and love towards them. He may become cruel and harsh, and child abuse may result.

The Visher study corroborates the Canadian finding of sexual tensions between stepparent and child. The authors note that, while it is difficult to obtain accurate data on the frequency of occurrence of sexual relationships between stepfathers and their stepdaughters, there are indications that a higher proportion of stepfathers are involved in such relationships than are natural fathers. The explanation for this is that 'the incest taboo is weakened because of the non-biological relationship between family members.'

It would be unwise to overstress the difficulties facing children in their relationship with a stepparent. In many cases the relationship can work out most satisfactorily. The study by Wallerstein and Kelly indicated that the remarriage of a parent 'enhanced the lives of many of the children, particularly those still in elementary school or younger. These children were better parented by happier mothers and by stepfathers who took their responsibility seriously and tried hard to fulfill a parental role.' Nevertheless, this study found that for approximately a quarter of the children, mostly those who were aged ten or older at the time of the remarriage, the needs of the youngsters diverged from those of the remarried parents. It also found that the rivalries between father and stepfather 'were often bitter and long lasting' and that these conflicts, which brought stepfather and mother on one side against the father, disturbed the child. The most tragic situations for the child were those where mother and stepfather demanded that the child renounce his or her love for the father as a price for acceptance and affection. This practice, described by Wallerstein and Kelly as 'scapegoating', sometimes (but not always) occurred where the child bore a physical resemblance to the father.

How does this evidence affect the debate on divorce? At first it might appear not to be greatly relevant since, whether there is a divorce jurisdiction or not, a second relationship may be formed. This is no doubt true, but the thrust of the argument in favour of divorce is that spouses should have the right to remarry: indeed this is the central difference between divorce and legal separation. This argument must not only contemplate the possibility of the formation of a second relationship, but also seek to facilitate its occurence. In the light of the evidence concerning the effects for children of the introduction of a stepparent into the home, it is surely only prudent, in the interests of children, to be aware of the possible difficulties that may result for them, while recognising the conflict of interests that may result for their parents.

CHAPTER 9

Reconciliation, Conciliation and the Family Court

> Most important, if divorce can be obtained easily even against op-
> position, it is essential that something positive should be done to
> provide conciliation services in order to save viable marriages, if
> only for the purpose of reaffirming in the face of the rising tide of
> divorces that the community continues to place its faith in the in-
> stitution of marriage as the basis of society.

With this statement Professor Hahlo of McGill University has
expressed a legitimate concern, which will be examined in this
chapter.

It is frequently suggested that a system of divorce based on
breakdown of marriage facilitates reconciliation between
spouses. It is said that instead of looking backwards and bicker-
ing about who did what, the spouses will look to the future
without acrimony and with some hope of becoming reconciled to
one another free from the shadow of recrimination. But is this
the way precedures for reconciliation have worked out in practice under divorce? Let us examine the position.

England

Detailed provisions regarding reconciliation were included in the
Divorce Reform Act 1969. Some well-meaning persons and
groups were impressed by these provisions: the National
Marriage Guidance Council, for example, 'warmly welcomed'
the statutory emphasis on reconciliation. Yet it was immediately
clear to those with special competence on the subject, and clear
to everyone else soon afterwards, that these provisions were
cosmetic rather than real – that they had been, in the words of
Dr Dominic Lasok, merely 'introduced as a palliative'. Michael
Freeman of London University, writing before the law had been
in operation, described them as 'a sham', and as 'half-hearted,
toothless and in their context useless', and David Morris
predicted that the provisions would not 'have any effect what-
soever.'

Within two years the National Marriage Guidance Council
was forced to revise its view of the provisions, their shortcomings
having become apparent to them. By then, the requirements for
reconciliation were regarded as rather tiresome formalities by

many solicitors and clients. A leading authority, Joseph Jackson, stated the position frankly in 1973 – a mere two years after the legislation had come into force: 'The fact is that the reconciliation provisions are a dead letter.'

The reconciliation provisions permit the Court to adjourn divorce proceedings at any stage if it appears that there is a reasonable possibility of reconciliation. Professor Bromley, speaking eight years after this provision had come into effect, said that he had never heard of a court actually exercising this power. He said further that the introduction of the 'Special Procedure' – that is, postal divorce – had 'certainly deprived the . . .provision of any effect.' He described the provision requiring the solicitor acting for the petitioner to certify whether he had discussed the possibility of reconciliation with him in these words: 'In practice this is a dead letter.'

Australia

The position in Australia was found to be exactly the same. Provisions for reconciliation were included in Part III of the *Matrimonial Causes Act 1959*. Proponents of the divorce legislation expressed confidence that these provisions would be effective. Unfortunately, as was the case in England, the promise was unfulfilled.

Judge Barber of the Supreme Court of Victoria described the reconciliation provisions as 'virtually useless in practice.' Professor Henry Finlay writing in 1969 explained that most solicitors regarded them as 'a mere formality which they are not obliged to comply with'; only twelve referrals for reconciliation were made throughout all of Australia under the statutory procedure over a period of eight years from the end of 1960 to the end of 1968. Summarising the effectiveness of the reconciliation provisions in 1974, Professor Finlay stated that they 'did not, as it turned out, go much beyond pious hopes'.

Neville Turner, speaking in 1976, described the reconciliation provisions as:

> a dead letter; a political compromise, designed to appease those legislators who felt uneasy about the great extension of grounds, and in particular the introduction of voluntary separation.

And he stated:

if the purpose of [the reconciliation provisions] was to reduce the divorce rate or even to stem the tide it has been hopelessly unsuccessful.

The *Family Law Act* of 1975 contains reconciliation provisions similar to those in English divorce law. All the weaknesses of the English approach have been perpetuated in the Australian scheme of conciliation. Commenting on the Australian provisions, Frank Bates has stated that

It is hard to see why these provisions should prove to be more successful than the much criticised equivalents in the 1959 Act [in Australia] and in England.

Canada
In Canada the position is no different. The reconciliation provisions in the *Divorce Act 1968* were criticised during the parliamentary debates on the legislation as being weak and rather meaningless – a prediction which proved to be only too accurate. The Canadian Law Reform Commission in its Working Paper on Divorce reports that 'experience has shown that [the reconciliation] provisions have failed to achieve their objective of promoting reconciliation.' Professor Howard and Barbara Irving state that: 'in effect the reconciliation clause was an exercise in futility, as it was almost a foregone conclusion that it would fail'.

South Africa
The *Divorce Act 1979* contains reconciliation provisions but the commentators have few illusions as to their probable effectiveness. Hahlo and Sinclair consider that, if the experience of other countries is any guide, 'there is little ground for optimism as to the success of attempts at reconciliation, but there are no doubt cases where such attempts ought to be made.'

Europe
In Europe provisions for reconciliation have been included in the divorce legislation in most countries but they are generally ineffective.

In Denmark, where a consensual divorce is sought by administrative procedure, the spouses are asked whether they want to try reconciliation. Professor Hahlo reports that:

In ninety-nine cases out of a hundred, this is a mere formality that takes only two or three minutes. The spouses decline and the session proceeds.

Spouses in Norway manage to complete the reconciliation procedure even more quickly. When seeking a separation order as a preliminary to divorce, spouses are required to appear before a mediator, who asks them whether they are willing to attempt reconciliation. Professor Hahlo states:

> If, as is usually the case, their answer is in the negative, the mediator stamps a certificate to the effect that a reconciliation attempt has been made but has failed, a procedure which usually takes about a minute.

Not surprisingly, reconciliation procedures in Norway have been described as 'a big joke.'

In Sweden the divorce legislation of 1973 omitted the requirement of reconciliation provisions since they were considered an infringement on the concept of individual autonomy.

LESSONS FOR IRELAND

We have seen that the experience of countries with no-fault divorce is that the reconciliation provisions introduced in the no-fault divorce legislation simply have not worked. Of course, it is difficult to see how it was ever believed that one could easily harmonize the conflicting philosophies of facilitating unilateral repudiation of a spouse and children on the one hand, and encouraging a joint commitment to resolve marital difficulties on the other. When legislation says to a man that, if he walks out on his wife and children, he will be entitled to a divorce, which in turn will reduce or eliminate his obligation to maintain a family, the prospects of successful conciliation are indeed bleak. Reconciliation procedures represent merely a nuisance – a troublesome hurdle to be crossed before the divorce decree is granted. Frank Bates, of the University of Tasmania, has appropriately captured the approach of the no-fault divorce philosophy towards reconciliation when, after a review of reconciliation provisions in Australia's divorce legislation, he states that:

> it would seem reasonable that impediments should not be placed in the way of dissolution so that parties will have the opportunity to achieve more satisfactory relationships with other people.

Frank Bates, after a review of the various reconciliation provisions in different no-fault divorce jurisdictions (including England, the United States, Australia and New Zealand) spells out the position with refreshing frankness:

> The chances, therefore, of any of the kind of reconciliation provisions considered above working effectively must be regarded as slight. Yet, legislators continue to include them. Reluctantly, the present writer is forced to the conclusion . . . that many of these provisions are included as a sop to the opponents of divorce reform. At the very most, recent instances can be regarded as manifestation of a desperate hope that, although others have failed, the most recent will succeed. There is little hard evidence to support any such optimism.

Judge Harlow Lenon, of Oregon, is equally frank. He observes that reconciliation provisions in the United States are:

> a crust to throw in placation to the opponents of quick no-fault divorce.

In our context, does this therefore mean that attempts at promoting reconciliation are futile and should not be backed by the law or given social or economic support? Surely not. Indeed there is unquestionably a pressing need for the marriage counselling agencies which already do valuable work in the community to receive far more assistance, so that they may enlarge and improve further their activities. It would be money well spent for the State to invest further in the training of personnel selected by these agencies, in the provision of substantial economic and educational resources, and supplementing existing facilities to cater for those spouses who might not be attracted to agencies organised on denominational lines.

Since it is generally accepted that the conciliation process tends to serve little useful function in encouraging reconciliation in cases where the spouses have already reached the courtroom, it seems desirable for social policy to concentrate on encouraging the spouses to embark on counselling far earlier than that. This policy should be stressed in the education of the public on the subject. Moreover, there would appear to be some advantage in ensuring that certain key persons including doctors, clergy and social workers, are particularly familiar with the work of the counselling agencies. These are the people likely to learn of marital difficulties at an early stage, in circumstances where there may well be a relationship of mutual trust.

Lawyers tend to have a somewhat different relationship with clients who have matrimonial difficulties. Some lawyers may regard themselves as best serving their client's interests if they act as an efficient 'hired gun' and seek to abstract the best deal possible from the other spouse; others may pay more attention to encouraging a reconciliation. The experience in other countries, as we have seen, is that provisions requiring lawyers to bring the existence of conciliation agencies to the attention of their clients have by and large not proved successful: most lawyers tend to regard them as little more than tiresome formalities. There seems to be no objection to including similar provisions in our law but it would be unwise to expect that in themselves they would have any substantial effect.

What would be more likely to prove successful in the long run is for the legal profession to learn more about how the counselling agencies operate and about the practical details of what is involved for the spouses. The Law Society has an excellent record in the field of continuing legal education – indeed it recently published information on the subject of matrimonial conselling in its *Gazette*. There would seem to be much to be said in favour of the State subsidising seminars and short courses run by the Law Society in order to make practitioners more fully aware of what the matrimonial counselling agencies have to offer.

Reconciliation or conciliation?

Of course, as is now more widely appreciated, there is a difference between *reconciliation,* which brings an estranged or disharmonious couple together again in a harmonious relationship, and *conciliation,* which eases the path to separation or divorce. Those who work in counselling, whatever their value-preference on issues of marital therapy, seem to be agreed that in some cases it will not be possible to bring about reconciliation: in these cases, conciliation can offer much comfort and help for the spouses. There have been locally organised conciliation schemes in Britain – the Bristol scheme being the most well-known – which have produced impressive results for their clients in easing the pain of dicorce and in some cases reconciling the spouses. The English Law Commission has recommended that a Committee be established to examine the possibility of similar schemes being organised on a national basis. This is a positive development which could well improve the position in England in coming years.

The family court

Discussion of these matters leads us inevitably to the question of court structures in relation to family law. Much criticism has been made in recent years of certain aspects of present structures. The notion of a family court is gradually taking shape. There is clearly room for reform of judicial structures, to reduce bitterness between the spouses, facilitate conciliation (or, if possible, reconciliation) and reduce the trauma for the parties and their children. We should closely monitor the experiments in other countries in relation to the family court, and more broadly, in relation to such important matters as the control of family violence, protection of the interests of children in proceedings affecting their welfare and parental guardianship and custody of children. But we do not need to wait for the results of experiments abroad. We are perfectly free to engage in our own research on these matters. So far the will appears to have been lacking. The current debate about divorce should serve as a catalyst for action.

CHAPTER 10

Divorce, Justice and the Courts

One of the principal consequences of divorce based on breakdown of marriage is that divorce ceases in practice to be a judicial procedure and becomes instead merely an administrative process, similar to a licensing procedure. Two dangers attaching to such a development are that divorces may be granted in cases where the marriage is still viable and that the question of justice and fairness between the parties may no longer be effectively taken into consideration.

When divorce based on breakdown of marriage was proposed in many countries, the proponents of this system went to considerable lengths to assure the public that the divorce process would remain essentially a judicial one. The only change in this regard, it was said, would be that the fault-based grounds for divorce would be replaced (or supplemented) by a new no-fault ground, namely that the marriage had irretrievably broken down. Inded the Court's proposed functions in adjudicating on important issues of justice between the spouses were particularly stressed by the supporters of no-fault divorce.

But the essence of the ground of irretrievable breakdown is that it is devoid of a substantial conceptual content capable of effective resolution in judicial proceedings. The Courts have struggled in vain to retain the illusion that they are performing a judicial function in granting divorces. But increasingly there is a trend towards admitting that the present judicial framework (so far as it has not already been superceded by an administrative machinery) is no more than what Michael Freeman of London University describes as 'a sham'.

No-fault divorce means that either spouse or both spouses may terminate the marriage at will. In this system there is no room for effective judicial intervention. As we have seen, any provisions included in divorce legislation which apparently give the court the power to adjudicate on whether or not a decree should be granted have turned out in practice to be completely ineffective, because they are inconsistent with the true meaning of divorce by unilateral repudiation. Professor Cary de Bessonet of Louisiana State University reports that

> Anyone who has witnessed an uncontested no-fault divorce or
> separation proceeding in court must be instantly stricken by the

absence of effective deterrents to intentional distortions of facts by the testifying party or corroborating witnesses. The proceeding generally bears an almost embarrassing resemblance to a well rehearsed play rather than a trial on the merits, with parties and witnesses uttering prepared responses to the guiding direction of their attorney. Such a proceeding is far from the process of truth solicitation that it is intended to be.

Divorce by post

The experience in England is instructive. When the *Divorce Reform Act 1969* was being enacted, the proponents of the legislation stressed that the divorce process should remain judicial rather than administrative - in other words, that the *Court* should have control over the proceedings rather than making the granting of a divorce akin to the granting of a licence. Within a few years, however, a Special Procedure was introduced, whereby divorces by consent may, in effect, be obtained *by post*.

The Special Procedure whereby one may obtain a divorce by post is a quaint example of legal formalism. The petitioner fills in a form without the right to legal aid although legal advice may be availed of where a means test has been satisfied. If the respondent does nothing, the form is placed with others in a pile for the 'day of the divorce.' There is no need for either spouse to attend court. The judge normally pronounces decrees for divorce 'in bulk', the judge simply saying, 'I pronounce decree *nisi* in cases 1 to 50.' Six weeks later, (or sooner in some cases) the spouses are free to remarry.

The Special Procedure was introduced in 1973. It was originally confined to undefended cases in which there were no children, based solely on the ground of two years' separation. In 1975 it was extended to undefended divorces on all grounds, except that of unreasonable behaviour. In 1977 it was extended to all undefended cases, including that of unreasonable behaviour, whether or not children were involved. At the same time the right to legal aid was withdrawn from special procedure cases; aid, however, remains available for ancillary matters and legal advice is also obtainable without charge.

A weakness associated with turning divorce into an administrative process is that it increases the likelihood of a marriage being dissolved where the relationship between the parties has not broken down. John Westcott stated in 1978 that

most practitioners have seen . . . petitions containing the flimsiest of particulars and one wonders how many of these petitions go through 'on the nod', as it were, simply because the respondents do not know what to do (and perhaps even believe that there is nothing they can do) when they are told that legal aid is not available to them to defend. Do all those petitions really present irretrievable breakdown situations?

In 1981, Mr Westcott expanded on this problem. He stated

> There is no duty upon the court to inquire whether there is an irretrievable breakdown; indeed no machinery for there to be an objective test of irretrievability exists under the law. In practice, the vast majority of divorces go through unilaterally and, with the advent of the special procedure, one suspects that there may be a significant number of respondents who, although feeling that there may not yet be an irretrievable breakdown, simply do not know how to stop or arrest the process. In consequence many feel that the State, through the courts, has no particular interest in finding out whether the marriage has in truth completely broken down.

Professor Bromley, also writing in 1981, noted that, under the Special Procedure, the provisions in the legislation relating to reconciliation 'are now completely meaningless'.

The judges themselves freely accept that the introduction of the Special Procedure has interfered with basic principles of justice. In a recent decision, Sir John Arnold, P. stated: 'So limited are the powers of the Judge concerned under the Rules that he has no real opportunity of investigating in depth what it is that substantial justice requires . . . .'

Other serious abuses of justice can result from the Special Procedure. Professor Bromley has noted that

> there is indeed little to stop a petitioner prepared to commit a flagrant act of perjury from obtaining a decree based on desertion or separation long before the relevant period of separation has elapsed.

Clearly, where divorce is obtained by the spouses filling in a form, with no attendance in court and without any meaningful investigation of the facts, it is implausible to suggest that divorce is still a judicial process in England. The English Law Commission in Working Paper No. 76 has recognised that the final pronouncement of a divorce by a judge cannot be regarded as more than a formality: and the granting of a divorce decree has thus become, in uncontested cases, an essentially administrative act.

Michael Eekelaar developed on this theme in 1978:

Essentially divorce has become an administrative process. Sentiment is satisfied by the solemn pronouncement of decree by a judge in a (possibly empty) courtroom. The choice of 'grounds' by the parties is simply part of the ritual. It has not the slightest relevance to the social or legal processes that take place.

Michael Freeman in 1976 analysed the development in frank terms:

The whole object of the Divorce Reform Act . . . . [is] a complete sham. Why, then, cannot we go the whole way and admit that postal divorce involves no adjudiciation and introduce 'post-office' divorce?

Lessons for Ireland

Let us summarise the effect of no-fault divorce on the judicial process. Since the Court has no real judicial function, it seems only logical that it should be replaced by an administrative 'post-office' system. But such a change enhances the risk that viable marriages may be terminated, as well as denying substantial justice to either or both of the spouses.

But can it not be argued that the effective abolition of judicial proceedings for divorce has some desirable effects? Does it not reduce the bitterness between the parties which contested judicial proceedings may involve? This highly desirable policy is frequently called in aid by those who seek to make consensual and unilateral divorce a matter of right with no judicial scrutiny. Indeed much of the recent international academic literature on the subject of divorce procedures suggests that proponents of liberal divorce are now placing as much confidence in the concept of 'mediation' between spouses as was placed in the concept of 'irretrievable breakdown of marriage' a decade ago.

We would all agree that court procedures and conciliation machinery should be geared so as to reduce to a minimum feelings of bitterness between the spouses. This is a most important area of reform, to which (as already mentioned) we should

give immediate priority. But we would be short-sighted if we failed to appreciate a rather obvious fact about human nature:
bitterness between spouses generally does not begin or end in a
court; it tends to be of longer-lasting dimensions, relating to
more intractable matters, including the behaviour and character
of spouses and the ability of the spouses to relate to each other
harmoniously.

The experience in countries with divorce shows that the enmi-
ty that may have existed between the spouses frequently does not
cease on divorce. The parties, whatever their marital status, in
many cases still have to keep in contact with each other, if only
as a means of keeping in touch with their children. There is
overwhelming evidence that these relationships are often
plagued with bitterness, and that the new wife does not regard
the position with any greater equanimity. The English Law
Commission in 1980 noted that the second wife resents having to
contribute to the former wife's support. It added: 'Not surprisingly this feeling is a cause of particular bitterness' where the
former wife has no children or does not herself work outside the
home. Conversely, the Commission noted that many divorced
wives 'resent their dependence' on State support at subsistence
level.

If divorce allegedly cures bitterness, one may ask why in
England in 1978 - several years after the *Divorce Reform Act 1969*
came into force - no fewer than 2,439 men went to prison for
wilful refusal or culpable negligence to pay maintenance. The
English Law Commission refers in this context to 'the bitterness
and resentment' surrounding the enforcement of financial
remedies. A possible explanation for this behaviour, which the
Commission appears to endorse, is that the men simply hated
their wives and were stubbornly prepared to undergo an infinite
number of prison sentence rather then pay a penny.

The international evidence therefore suggests that the removal
of divorce from the scrutiny of the court denies justice to the
spouses, without removing the bitterness which frequently
plagues the relationship of the spouses during and after their
marriage.

CHAPTER 11

Divorce and Marriage Stability

It seems reasonable to predict that legislation permitting unilateral divorce would have some destabilising effect on marriage. Marriage, after all, involves a commitment which at times is hard to live up to; almost all marriages have their difficult patches. It seems only consistent with common sense that if divorce is available as a tempting release from these difficulties, some spouses will be likely to resort to it even though, if they persevered, the difficulties might have been resolved. This risk is enhanced under a system of divorce based on breakdown of marriage, since under this system of divorce either spouse is entitled to a divorce without regard to the wishes of the other spouse.

Termination of viable marriages

Studies that have been carried out on modern divorce law in operation have confirmed that viable marriages may be terminated. We have already referred to an important study carried out by Judith Wallerstein and Joan Kelly into the operation of modern divorce in California. The results were reported in a book entitled *Surviving the Breakup* which was published in 1980. The findings of this study in relation to children have already been detailed. Let us now examine what it has to say on the question of the spouses' relationship with each other at the time of the divorce.

Wallerstein and Kelly found that:

> People opt for divorce for complex motives, some of which have little, if any, relation to marital incompatibility.

Wallerstein and Kelly identified several types of divorce which were not the result of marital unhappiness on the part of either spouse. The first was where the decision to divorce followed upon some stressful experience outside the marriage which was profoundly upsetting to the person who then initiated the move towards divorce. 'The response to the external stress, in other words, ricocheted into the family area.' Experiences that induced such divorce included the unexpected death of a grandparent, the diagnosis of a mortal illness, or a crippling accident to a child. Wallerstein and Kelly explain that:

The psychological mechanisms that lead from such stress to divorce can be explained by the stressed person's need to take flight to ward off the depression that threatens to overwhelm him or her. Thus, the same tragedy that has the potential to mobilize some families, drawing the members closer together in mutual support, paradoxically has the potential to rupture other families, as one or both parents escape from each other and run from the tragedy and so avert the threatened depression.

The decision to divorce at such an inappropriate time serves only further to diminish the supports available in the family, when such supports are the most sorely needed of all.

Wallerstein and Kelly report that:

> The children are burdened especially, since the divorce makes no sense, brings no relief to any identified family conflict, and the pain of the family disruption only adds to the awful pain of the family's initial unhappiness.

A case studied by the authors concerned a woman who filed for divorce shortly after her mother died. Her husband, who was a devoted family man, was startled and begged her to change her mind, or at least to permit him to remain within the family home, since he had no place to go. The children implored their mother to change her mind. Four years later, the woman told Drs. Wallerstein and Kelly:

> 'I wish I could marry him again. I was upset. My mother had died, and I felt that he wasn't sympathetic, and I filed for divorce. It was a terrible mistake, but there is nothing to do now. I have ruined the lives of four people.'

The authors identify another form of divorce which reflected stress: this is a divorce that is linked to the severe psychological illness of the parent filing for divorce. The authors report that:

> Several adults in the study developed a sudden rash of symptomatic behaviour which included their decision to divorce as one of the new symptoms. Some of these decisions occurred within the context of an ongoing marriage that other family members assumed was satisfactory, even happy. These divorce requests, coming from persons in the throes of severe psychiatric illness, were often tragic because if the person who sought the divorce

was successful, he or she was separated from family support exactly when it was most needed. An additional complication was the fact that the person who was decompensating often showed other bizarre behaviour at the same time, and the children were therefore confronted simultaneously with a disturbed parent and ruptured marriage.

Drs Wallerstein and Kelly report that the families in which divorce was sought by an emotionally disturbed parent often did not identify the behaviour as disturbed or as constituting a psychiatric illness. The children in these families and the spouse who opposed the divorce decision were often bewildered and distraught. Morever, since the decision to divorce did not address any particular problems within the marriage, there was no relief or sense of closure after the divorce.

Another group of divorces discovered by Drs Wallerstein and Kelly were those undertaken without reflection or planning or any real consideration of the consequences. One example of these impulsive divorces was where divorce was employed as a strategy by the aggrieved husband or wife to punish the partner involved in an extramarital affair and to try in this way to return the partner to the marriage. Several women sued for divorce in outrage and jealousy, yet secretly hoped to win back their husbands with this manoeuvre. 'Mostly, if not always,' this strategy failed. The authors found that:

> One consequence of the use of divorce as a weapon to punish the errant spouse is that the aggrieved partner may continue to rage for years. Furthermore, since the intent was to employ the divorce primarily as a strategy to restore the marital tie, the parting brought a lessened capacity and little motivation to the complex tasks of the divorcing period.

We must keep these findings in a proper perspective. It is clear from Wallerstein and Kelly's study that in many cases divorce was not undertaken impulsively: indeed many of the spouses 'had been locked into marriages in which for a long time they had been demeaned, neglected and abused, and the decision to divorce had by no means been taken lightly. Often it had been delayed long past the point when it seemed the proper and inevitable step to resolve their own life unhappiness.'

In attempting to apply these findings in the Irish context, we should of course be cautious. An impetuous decision to separate, in a country where there is no divorce, may result in subsequent regret, just as it does in countries with divorce. New relationships may have been formed by the time one partner has second thoughts; by this time it may be too late to undo the damage. Nevertheless, the fact remains that where divorce is obtainable by consent or demand, there must always remain the possibility that essentially viable marriage relationships will be terminated. We have already seen how commentators in England have noted, that under modern divorce law, viable marriages may be terminated. It will be recalled that John Westcott has stated of the present 'postal divorce' there that:

> most practitioners have seen . . . petitions containing the flimsiest of particulars and one wonders how many of these petitions go through 'on the nod', as it were, simply because the respondents do not know what to do (and perhaps even believe that there is nothing they can do) when they are told that legal aid is not available to them to defend. Do all those petitioners really present irretrievable breakdown situations?

Moreover we have also seen that Mr Westcott, writing in 1981, stated that:

> In practice, the vast majority of divorces go through unilaterally and, with the advent of the special procedure, one suspects that there may be a significant number of respondents who, although feeling that there may not yet be an irretrievable breakdown, simply do not know how to stop or arrest the process. In consequence many feel that the State, through the courts, has no particular interest in finding out whether the marriage has in truth completely broken down.

Many commentators have made the point that the creation or expansion of legal availability of divorce is damaging to the stability of marriage. Thus Professor Henry Finlay, one of Australia's foremost academic family lawyers, stated five years ago that the extension of the grounds for divorce in legislation in that country is a 'further contributing cause in the further increase in the divorce-proneness in our society.' Writing in 1970, Professor Finlay expressed the view that it was 'no doubt perfectly true' that divorce based on consent 'would destroy the whole basis of our society, marriage and the family.' He added that 'it seems to be becoming increasingly clear that divorce, once permitted, does not provide for half measures.'

On similar lines Kathleen Heasman of London University stated four years ago that family breakdown 'is more common today than it was in the past. This is partly because . . . divorce is now far easier.'

Clifford Kirkpatrick states:

> It can even be argued that divorce itself is a cause of divorce, in that frequent divorce weakens the norm of marital stability. Divorce frees bad matrimonial risks for remarriage and subsequent divorce: offspring imitate divorced parents; and the divorce of numerous friends makes the choice of divorce more normal and respectable.

In Canada, the Special Joint Committee of the Senate and the House of Commons, in its Report on Divorce in 1967, stated that:

> Divorce by consent would tend to affect the dissolution of marriages that had not really broken down or been destroyed. Unless some test or provision was introduced to determine this fact, there is the likelihood that many couples would rush into divorce without really giving their marriage a chance to work or without trying to work out what might well be soluble problems.

This point is echoed by the Scottish Law Commission in its Report on Divorce in 1967 (para. 12):

> We believe that a provision for divorce by consent would inevitably shake the resolution of permanance with which marriages are now entered into, and encourage a less responsible attitude; this would not only be contrary to the policy of the community, but would be unacceptable to public opinion.

Similarly C.M. Butler, of the University of Sydney, states that he finds it 'difficult to believe' that legislation permitting divorce by mutual consent would not 'drastically alter approaches to marriage'. He argues that:

> Legislation on these lines, although it would not amount to equating the marriage ceremony with ordinary contracts, would surely inevitably alter its traditional image . . . . The tremendous psychological influence on the populus which legislation undoubtedly has, should be exercised with the utmost discretion and restraint . . .

Although [the three-year bar to divorce] would probably prevent the emergence of a practice of 'trial marriages', there would
nevertheless be a reduction in belief in the sanctity of marriage.
The effect would not merely be to make divorce easier . . . but to
make it available without any grounds whatever where both
parties agree. In other words it would no longer even purport to
be anything more than an administrative affair. It is important to
note that any change in attitude would not be immediate but
would develop over a number of years.

There are, of course, commentators who have argued that the
divorce laws have no practical effect on marriage stability. The
most prominent of these was the late Professor Max Rheinstein
of the University of Chicago. Rheinstein's thesis has been un-
critically accepted by some authors but when subjected to close
analysis by leading scholars it has proved to be seriously defec-
tive. A detailed discussion of Rheinstein's thesis and of the
available data is made in Appendix A of *Divorce and Social Policy*.

Cohabitation outside marriage

The experience of countries with divorce based on breakdown of
marriage is that cohabitation outside marriage has increased.
Freeman and Lyons explain the growing popularity of non-
marital cohabitation in England as being caused in part by
'easier divorce so that marriage is no longer any guarantee of
permanence.' Similarly Stuart explains that virtually identical
changes in Scottish divorce legislation have 'undoubtedly . . .
played their part in permitting the view to develop that there is
little point in marrying where almost immediate divorce application is possible . . . ' So also in the United States, where cohabitation outside marriage has been rapidly increasing, Glick and
Spanier have stated that, among other factors

> the increasing liberalization of norms relating to life styles . . . and
> the decrease in social stigma associated with divorce, undoubted-
> ly make cohabitation a relatively attractive and plausible tem-
> porary life style for some.

In Sweden, the law of divorce, already liberal, was made still
more liberal in 1973, in order to encourage couples contemplating cohabitation outside marriage to marry instead. The
belief of the legislators was that if divorce was extremely easy
this would make marriage less frightening for these couples. Ex-

perience has, however, shown that the easy divorce law has not resulted in a substantial increase in marriage, and a decrease in cohabitation. Rather, the reverse phenomena have occurred. In 1969, the share of unmarried couples in the total number of cohabiting couples was estimated at 6-7%. According to the population and housing census of 1975 the share had risen to more than 11%, a figure which may, however, be thought rather too low in view of the fact that the existence of cohabitation is probably not always revealed. In 1978 the proportion was estimated as having risen to 15%, and a further rise is likely to have occurred since 1978.

The problem in perspective

It is, of course, very difficult indeed to determine precisely the effect of divorce legislation on marriage stability. There are problems in abstracting what are the strictly legal influences from the broader social spectrum. Very few studies have attempted this process of abstraction, no doubt because it is a dauntingly difficult task. Most of the studies that have been carried out were of societies different in time and place from our own society today; some of the studies, by virtue of their terms of reference, could not answer the question we would wish to pose. Nevertheless, so far as these studies throw any light on this problem, they do not refute and in some respects support the commonsense judgement of human nature - that, if divorce is available, it is likely to have some destabilising effect on marriage.

Of course, this is not to suggest that other factors do not have an important effect on marriage stability: obviously they do. Such aspects as pre-marital pregnancy, religious difference, age and educational achievement play an important role, as well as more general considerations such as urbanisation, industrialization, and the cultural attitudes of the community to divorce.

No one is so naive as to believe that complete marriage stability can be ensured by prohibiting divorce; equally no one believes that divorce law is the only cause of marriage breakdown. But if divorce legislation leads to the breakdown of some marriages that would otherwise have succeeded this is a most serious consequence to which great weight should quite clearly be attached.

CHAPTER 12

Is Divorce the Answer?

It is now time to return to the question raised at the beginning of this book. Is divorce legislation a humane solution to the problem of marital disharmony and disruption? We cannot attempt to answer this question without, first, setting out the main findings of our research, and secondly, considering their implications in the context of Ireland. Moreover, we must constantly bear in mind that the problem of marital disharmony and disruption in this country will not in any way be reduced if we conclude that the introduction of divorce would not be desirable. We should honestly recognise the extent of this problem, which requires a social and legal response. Ultimately the question must involve a *choice* between divorce, on the one hand, and some other range of social and legal responses, on the other. It is not sufficient to establish that divorce would have detrimental consequences for our society: before rejecting divorce we must be satisfied that these detrimental consequences would be worse than the social and personal implications of marriage disruption in a divorceless society.

The findings of our research on divorce

Let us summarise briefly the main findings from our research. We have seen, first, that divorce based on breakdown of marriage results in women being divorced in circumstances of real hardship. This is the universal experience in countries which have introduced this system of divorce, and the legal commentators accept that any attempt to protect wives against being divorced in cases where the divorce would cause hardship is contrary to the philosophy of no-fault divorce.

We have also seen that no-fault divorce results in the tendency to reduce the amount of support that divorced wives receive from their husbands. Again, the concept of divorce based on breakdown of marriage tends to run counter to many women's interests, since its underlying philisophy can only operate effectively where men are relieved of their full economic responsibilities towards their former wives.

We have seen that the existing rights of married women in relation to the family home would also be likely to be restricted under no-fault divorce, as they have already been reduced in countries which have adopted no-fault divorce. Moreover, we have seen that women's succession rights tend to be damaged under a modern divorce system.

As regards children, the prospect is equally daunting. The experience of countries which have adopted a system of divorce based on breakdown of marriage is that the detailed provisions included in the divorce legislation for the purpose of providing some protection for the interests of children have, in fact, proved virtually useless. Moreover, there are disturbing trends towards reducing the obligations of fathers to support their children, especially where the fathers are no longer living with their children and have little continuing contact with them; the philosophy of no-fault divorce means that the father as well as the child should be regarded as a 'casualty' of a broken marriage; and why should one casualty be obliged to support another?

The formerly prevalent conception of divorce as therapeutic is, as we have noted, becoming difficult to reconcile with a substantial and growing volume of clinical experience of doctors, psychologists and psychiatrists which indicates that many children suffer considerable fear, depression, anger and guilt from their experience of parental separation. Moreover we have seen how the relationship between stepparent and stepchild may suffer from loyalty conflicts, sexual tension and other difficulties.

We have seen how, under a system of divorce bases on breakdown of marriage, proceedings tend to become increasingly more administrative than judicial, with the result that considerations of justice between the spouses, or between the parents and the children, can less easily be taken into account. In this context, we have found that reconciliation provisions included in no-fault legislation have proved almost without exception to be useless formalities, and that there is a clear risk of viable marriages being terminated.

Lessons for Ireland

With this picture of divorce it is difficult to conclude that the humanitarian case for divorce is a strong one. But this does not mean that no humanitarian case can be put forward, notwithstanding the evidence which we have analysed in detail. It may be argued first that, although of course we should have regard to the international experience of modern divorce, we should not conclude fatalistically that what happened abroad would necessarily also happen here. Surely we can learn from the mistakes in other countries so as to produce a just and workable system of divorce for our people? This line of argument obviously has some force but it fails to give sufficient weight to the inherent logic of a system of divorce based on marriage breakdown. Generally the unpalatable effects of this system of divorce have not resulted because of a *misapplication* of the law but precisely because these effects are the *necessary implications* of divorce based on breakdown of marriage. We have seen how the commentators accept that this is so. In this country, therefore, when deciding whether or not we should introduce divorce, we are in the advantageous position that we can see beyond the slogans to the real issues. We are faced with a stark choice, and if we choose divorce, we will do so with the clear know dge of its effects for spouses, children and society. This is a luxury that has been denied to the electorates of other countries.

Problems for a divorceless society

In spite of the unpalatable consequences of divorce it can be argued that the *absence* of divorce in a society creates its own hardships and injustice. It has been pointed out that children of second unions, who would be legitimate if divorce were permitted, are illegitmate where no divorce is allowed. This argument can be shortly disposed of. There is no need to resort to a system of divorce to cure the problem of illegitimacy. A far simpler and more just solution is to be preferred. This is for the enactment of legislation entirely abolishing the status of illegitimacy for *all* children born outside marriage. This matter will be discussed in more detail later. But in the present context, the point to be noted is that divorce would not adequately resolve the problem of illegitimacy. It would only afford a partial solution, since it would do nothing to improve the status of children whose parents never married. There is, moreover, evidence from other countries, where liberal divorce was introduced to enable parties of second unions to marry and thus legitimate their children, that such parties tend to be slow to avail themselves of the opportunity. Stephen Cretney, of the English Law Commission, after a review of English experience, concluded in 1979 that 'it does seem that the expectation of the promoters of the Divorce Reform Act 1969 that easier divorce would reduce the number of illegitimate children living with their parents in stable unions has not been fulfilled.'

In favour of introducing divorce it can be argued that, under the existing position, where divorce is not permitted, a woman whose marriage has failed and who enters into a second union is deprived of the opportunity to obtain legally enforceable rights of maintenance against her new partner. The absence of divorce can thus be regarded as working against the financial interests of a woman placed in such circumstances. Where. for example, a young woman had been deserted early in her marriage, she would be able to contemplate the security of entering a second marriage if divorce were permitted. There is force in this argument. On close scrutiny, however, it is somewhat less impressive than it may at first appear. Although it is true that divorce would result in greater financial security for some women, it is also the case that where their new partners had already been married, this greater financial security would be gained at the expense of *other* women, the former wives of these men. In some cases it may be predicted that the balance of the equities would favour this outcome but as a general social policy it would be likely to have unsatisfactory and unjust results which would outweigh the benefits in individual cases. We have only to think of the older wife, discarded by her husband in favour of a younger, unmarried, woman. If divorce were permitted her husband could say to her: 'After I divorce you, do not fear: you can always secure your financial position by marrying again, if someone will have you.' Moreover, as we have seen, divorce subverts rather than supports the maintenance obligations of marriage. Men's obligations to support their divorced wives have been radically reduced, and in some cases abrogated, and the thrust is to reduce these obligations further. If we are concerned about the financial security of women, therefore, international experience shows that we would be acting imprudently in introducing divorce.

Developing further the theme of economic dependency, it may be argued that, in spite of the difficulties for many women which no-fault divorce involves, some women will not suffer hardship at all by being divorced: they may be in well-paid full-time employment outside the home, or, at the other end of the economic scale, they may already be depending exclusively on social welfare payments. The experience of countries with no-fault divorce is that women in increasing numbers are seeking divorce: clearly these women, on balance, consider that divorce offers more to them than remaining married. Undoubtedly, the changes in employment patterns and sex roles have contributed to making divorce a more attractive option for some women, but, as we have seen, it is also the case that for many other women divorce represents an economic threat.

The overall picture that emerges from the international evidence is that, even in industrial societies far more advanced than our own, divorced women in large numbers continue to experience severe economic hardship: indeed, all the evidence suggests that as long as traditional structures of family relationships continue to exist, even in attenuated form, divorced wives will suffer hardship.

For several reasons divorce does not appear capable of resolving the problems for women which arise in Irish society where cultural values regarding sex roles are gradually changing. First, as we have seen, in such a culture no-fault divorce leaves behind it a mass of casualties in the form of women and children who suffer economic hardship. Second, no-fault divorce will continue to create these casualties for as long as traditional family structures remain. In Ireland these may last for a considerable time. Moreover, as we have already mentioned, it is probable that many of those who would support the introduction of divorce as a humane solution may not fully appreciate that, if divorce is not to harm women and children, it must involve radical changes in family structures and sex roles. It is far from certain that, when this reality becomes clearer to them, these people would necessarily be willing to support these radical structural changes. If they do not fully accept them - and experience abroad suggests that they will not do so within the short or medium term – divorced wives and their children will be the casualties. Finally, a basic question of justice arises in relation to the many thousands of women who belong to families structured along traditional lines. Whatever may be in store for our society in the long term as far as sex roles are concerned, is it fair to these women to cause them the hardship which experience elsewhere strongly suggests will be caused by divorce?

At various times proposals have been made in some countries to resolve the problem of economic hardship for divorced wives, through either public subsidies or some form of 'divorce insurance.' In England public subsidies were favoured by the Finer Report in 1974 but were rejected by the (Labour) Government on the basis that the country could not afford it. In New Zealand there is a Domestic Purposes Benefit, not dissimilar in some respects to our deserted wives benefit, but applying to a wider category of women. This has been supplemented by a 'liable parents contribution scheme,' introduced by the *Social Security Amendment Act 1980*. The effect of the scheme is to transform the determination of financial support by parents of their children into a matter for an administrative decision made by officers of the Social Security Commission (with wide-ranging administrative powers of enforcement and investigation) rather than remaining a matter for judicial determination by the Court.

These proposals, if put into effect, would be likely to go some way towards mitigating the hardship suffered by divorced women, but a realistic assessment of experience in countries with divorce would suggest that they are not likely to remove the hardship caused by divorce. Already in Ireland we have a system of state support for women whose marriages are disrupted by desertion. An expansion of this system could clearly relieve the plight of women who became economic victims of no-fault divorce. Indeed there is a strong argument for extending this benefit to all families. But economic realities suggest that the public purse will not be the total answer. The experience in other countries is that social welfare entitlements for divorced women are not unduly generous. For some women, of course, state payments would not represent a loss of income - indeed they might represent an increase - but for many others, especially where the family income before the divorce was a good one, the. state payments would go only some way towards mitigating their loss. Again we must be realistic: whether or not divorce is introduced, many families will suffer economically from marriage disruption. It normally costs more for spouses to live apart than together and the economic resources of families generally do not extend to the extra costs.

Is a restricted form of divorce the solution?

We now must consider whether a *restricted* form of divorce would be acceptable. We must ask ourselves not only whether a particularly restricted form seems *theoretically* defensible but also whether it would be likely to work out satisfactorily *in practice*. It has rightly been said that law involves 'social engineering': if our blueprint does not work out when put to the test in society, then it must be rejected, however attractive it may appear on paper.

Divorce by mutual consent?

Let us begin with divorce by mutual consent. The case for a system of divorce by mutual consent is clearly a good deal stronger than that for divorce at the demand of one spouse: if both spouses wish to leave each other and to remarry, what soical purpose is served by the law not giving effect to their wishes?

The balance of the social argument seems, however, to be against the introduction of divorce by consent. A number of factors have been identified by agencies which have examined this question. First, as the Canadian Special Joint Committee of the Senate and House of Commons has noted, there is the risk that divorce by consent 'would tend to effect the dissolution of marriages that had not broken down.' Certainly it would be difficult for the legislation to prevent this risk from arising: as we have seen, the experience of countries with divorce is not encouraging. Next, there is a real risk that the stronger partner will be able to get his or her way by economic or other pressures. At present, in many cases, the stronger partner will be the husband. The prospect of pressure being brought on wives by husbands is a real one: it occurred in *Gaffney v Gaffney,* a case decided by the Supreme Court in 1975, where a husband forced his wife by threats of physical violence to obtain a divorce in England against her wishes. There is today a growing awareness of the existence of wife battering and more generally of coercion in marriage relationships; the potential for hardship resulting from a consensual divorce law should not be ignored.

It would be possible, of course, for the law to attempt to ensure that a wife (and, indeed, a husband) freely consented to a divorce, but if one is realistic one must accept that such a procedure would not be likely to work effectively. Unless a very elaborate scheme were to be devised it would be difficult to unearth cases of duress. Certainly, it is unlikely that any scheme, however complex, would be able to monitor cases where the consent of a wife was vitiated because her husband exercised a dominating influence over her, falling short of violence or the threat of violence. From a practical standpoint, one must seriously doubt that spouses would accept the thorough and searching enquiry into their personal lives which would be necessary if a serious attempt were to be made in the divorce legislation to ensure that the consent of both spouses to the divorce was freely given.

A third objection to divorce based on the consent of the spouses is that it would lead to serious anomalies: it would mean, for example, that a divorce could not be obtained where an adulterer or wife-beater did not consent to be divorced. This anomaly could be removed only by the creation of the more fundamental anomalies which would result from the inclusion of *fault* grounds for divorce as well as the ground of consent of the spouses.

A further objection to the ground of consent of the spouses is that it ignores the interests of the children. In the light of the evidence of damage to children which we have already considered, this is an important consideration. Whether or not we would wish it otherwise, there may be a conflict of interests between the divorce aspirations of one or both of the parents and the emotional tranquility of their children.

Divorce by consent for childless couples?

It has sometimes been suggested that, on this account, divorce should be available to *childless* couples only. This approach may commend itself to many people. If, for example, two young people marry and within a short time, before they have children, discover that they are totally incompatible, what social purpose is served by denying them the right to remarry? Surely a right to divorce in such limited circumstances would not be socially damaging? Indeed, is it not socially necessary?

But it seems likely that such a limited right to divorce would create its own difficulties. The English Law Commission in its Report on Divorce in 1967 was surely right in thinking that it would be undesirable 'to make the children the fulcrum on which their parents' hopes of a divorce would turn.' The most obvious drawback to permitting divorce for childless couples is that this would make every marriage a 'trial marriage,': pressures would be created on childless couples whose marriage got into difficulties to divorce before the option was removed by the birth of a child. Moreover, it would not be desirable for parents to perceive their children as a barrier to divorce: clearly, most parents would be sufficiently mature and fair not to blame their children but not all parents might take this attitude. One has only to think of the evidence of 'scape-goating' of children, revealed in Wallerstein and Kelly's study, to appreciate that parents are not always fair or rational in their treatment of their children. Nor should we ignore the realities of 'practical politics.' It is probable that, once divorce for childless couples had been introduced, pressure would immediately mount for an entension to couples with children. The dividing line would involve so many anomalies that it would be likely to be regarded as arbitrary and unjust. For example, a woman who was being battered by her husband would be denied a divorce (to which the husband consented) by reason only of the fact that the couple had children. Who would attempt to justify an anomaly such as this? Again the inclusion of a fault ground would only multiply the inconsistencies and anomalies.

Indeed the same point can also be made about any system of divorce based on consent. Once it had been accepted, it would be difficult not to yield to pressure for an extension to divorce at the demand of either spouse. Certainly, the thrust of the argument of those who press for the introduction of divorce is towards divorce based on irretrievable breakdown of marriage, including divorce at the demand of either spouse, rather than for a limited ground of divorce based on the consent of both spouses.

Having mentioned all these substantial practical objections to introducing a limited system of divorce based on consent, it should nonetheless be admitted that these objections will probably seem very foreign and uncompelling to some married couples who are living apart and wishing to be divorced. These couples may understandably feel aggrieved that, as they see it, in the interest of *other* couples they should be denied a divorce. Our humanitarian concern for these couples impels us towards giving them the relief which they seek. But the fact remains that social and legal policy on divorce does have significant social and interpersonal implications. We have already documented in detail the detrimental effects of these implications. The question thus is one involving a balance between the perceived injury of denying divorce to couples who want it, on the one hand, and the injury that will result for others if a system of divorce based on consent is introduced. The couples wanting divorce may argue that it is wrong for the law to deny them the relief they seek, in the interests of others: for why should they have to suffer to prevent injury to other persons, whom they do not know, and who will never appreciate the sacrifice that has been made on their behalf? This attitude is perfectly understandable but, on reflection, it will be seen that, from the standpoint of social policy, a broader perspective is required. Let us look at the children who would suffer from the introduction of divorce. Are they not also allowed to argue that *they* should not be required to suffer so that other persons may seek relief? Are not they allowed to point out that those seeking divorce will never appreciate the sacrifice that has been made on their behalf? The lesson we can learn from examining the problem from both of these standpoints is that it would be simplistic to argue for or against the introduction of divorce from the perspective of only one group of affected persons. The question can be resolved only after balancing the competing interests involved.

Is fault-based divorce the solution?

We must now consider whether a fault-based system of divorce would be appropriate. Under this system divorce would be permitted where a spouse could establish that the other spouse committed an act or acts in serious breach of his or her matrimonial responsibilities, such as adultery or cruelty. Fault-based divorce has few, if any, supporters today. Although such a system of divorce originally seemed to many people to have much to commend it, and was adopted by several countries, generally it was found to be unsatisfactory in its practical operation. It proved difficult to prevent divorces taking place by agreement, with perjured 'evidence' of misconduct being presented to the court. In more recent times the very notion of matrimonial fault as a ground for divorce has come under sustained attack by those who argue that difficulties in marriage relationships frequently are the result of either the fault of both spouses or of incompatibility of temperament. Moreover, it was argued that divorce based on fault grounds encouraged acrimony and hostility between the spouses, since it was in the interests of either to magnify the wrongs of the other.

It seems quite clear that a fault-based system of divorce simply is not a practical political possibility. Virtually no-one has recommended its introduction. On the contrary, the entire thrust of the argument of those who press for divorce is that divorce based on breakdown of marriage is the appropriate system. We should, however, be cautious lest, in the interests of political compromise, support grows for a *combined* system of divorce based on *both* fault and no-fault grounds. Whatever strategic attractions such a system might have *politically,* it could not be defended on social or legal grounds. Such a solution would almost certainly be only a temporary one, as experience in several other countries shows. Moreover, once the no-fault ground of breakdown of marriage had been introduced, the no-fault philosophy would tend to prevail.

The stark choice

It would seem, therefore, that whatever theoretical arguments may be made in their favour, limited no-fault, or fault-based, grounds for divorce are not realistic options. Whether or not we would wish it otherwise, the choice is ultimately a stark one: between marriage defined in terms of a binding lifelong commitment, on the one hand, with no divorce, and a system of divorce based on marriage breakdown on the other.

The social question

Let us examine the broader social aspects of this question. Whether or not divorce is a *humane* response to marriage disruption, perhaps it is nonetheless *socially necessary* in order to avoid the anomalies that the absence of divorce may entail? Some of these anomalies have already been identified in public discussion: *first,* where there is no divorce, children who are born of second unions are illegitimate and remain so, even if their parents marry each other after their spouses have died; *secondly,* religious annulments have no legal effect; and *thirdly,* it is argued that a significant incidence of second unions makes a mockery of the prohibition on divorce. Let us examine each of these issues in turn.

1. Illegitimate children and divorce

We have already considered the argument that divorce is necessary to resolve the problem of the illegitimacy of children of second unions. The solution to the problem of illegitimacy is to abolish the status of illegitimacy, not resort to divorce, which could only be a partial, less than effective and, in the present context, over-board legal response.

2. Religious marriage annulments

The second issue relates to the divergence between church and state on the question of religious marriage annulments. This issue extends, of course, beyond social questions into the heart of political controversy. As is frequently the case with church-state relations, it is difficult to find a solution that will satisfy all political viewpoints. Some people may consider it desirable that the marriage law of the state should not diverge substantially from the religious values of the majority; others, favouring a more pluralist approach, may argue that the state has no right to reflect in its laws the values of one religion rather than another. As was made clear in Chapter I, this book is concerned with the social argument relating to divorce: it is not concerned with political or religious questions. Therefore, some aspects of the argument just mentioned will not be pursued: these raise issues on which legitimate *political* debate may take place but which (although clearly having a social dimension) are not themselves social arguments.

So far as the *social* argument is concerned, two comments appear to be appropriate. The first is that the numerical extent of the problem is perhaps less extensive than public discussion might have suggested. The number of religious annulments granted annually throughout Ireland was negligible until 1974. In that year the figure rose sharply and until 1977 the annual average of annulments granted was around a hundred. Since then the numbers have been under a hundred each year. In 1982 eighty three annulments were granted. In the majority of cases, there was a prohibition on one or both of the parties against remarriage, subject to permission being granted only after a most thorough investigation of the person's capacity for a proposed marriage.

These statistics, as social phenomena, reveal a social problem of significant but scarcely massive proportions. In this context, the proposal to abolish the concept of illegitimacy, already mentioned, would be an important step in mitigating the detrimental effects.

In contemplating possible solutions to the problem of church-state relations on the question of annulment, one thing is certain: divorce is not the answer. If divorce were to be introduced to deal with the specific problem of religious annulments only, such legislation would almost certainly be met with sustained criticism on the basis that it involved religious discrimination and also on the basis that it failed to deal with those couples whose marriages were disrupted but who were not entitled to a religious annulment. It seems probable that legislation on these lines would be politically unacceptable. It is far more likely that a divorce system applying to *all* marriages would be introduced. This would mean that, to deal with the social problem of less than 100 religious annulments a year, every marriage would be exposed to the possibility of termination by divorce. This is surely overkill on a massive scale. One can only plead for political honesty in this sphere: if divorce is socially desirable for the community then we should have divorce for that reason, rather than because of the small but intractable social problem caused by religious annulments. Conversely, if divorce is not socially desirable for the community, its introduction can scarcely be justified on the basis of the difficulty about religious annulments. Introducing divorce would involve replacing one social problem by a far more serious and extensive one.

3. The growth of irregular unions

The next argument we must consider is that in our community there is a rising incidence of marriage breakdown which has resulted in the growth of second unions which, on account of the absence of divorce, cannot become marriages. It is said that this phenomenon puts our legal system into disrepute; divorce is perceived as desirable since it would remove the mockery and chaos which such a situation involves. This argument – if its factual elements can be established - clearly has some force. Let us assume for a moment a hypothetical society, the clear majority of whose members no longer regarded marriage as involving a lifelong commitment, in which permanent marriage relationships were the exception rather than the rule. In such circumstances what would be the proper attitude towards divorce? Would it be sufficient to reject divorce on the basis that it is not a humane response to marriage breakdown, involving as it does hardship and injustice to wives and children? Would not such a response be regarded as socially inadequate? It would understandably be criticised on the basis that it ignored the realities of the society in question. A system of divorce for such a society might well be considered *socially* necessary, in spite of the inhumanity and hardship it involves at a personal level. The social necessity would relate to the fact that the members of such a society, in their perceptions and the way they lived their lives, had clearly adopted a norm of impermanence in relationships, and had rejected the norm of permanence. For the law not to reflect this change in norms would be likely to result in its failure to deal adequately with the social realities in that society. On balance, therefore, the prudent decision might well be that, for that society, divorce (with all its problems) represented the lesser of two evils. But clearly this decision would only be reached where it was evident that all other options were manifestly unworkable, and where the social damage was very significant.

To what extent does our present society compare with the hypothetical society we have described? Unfortunately, there are considerable difficulties in giving a precise estimate of the incidence of marriage breakdown: census data have never been kept and other indicators can suggest only a provisional conclusion, since they do not accurately reflect the incidence of breakdowns.

Least accurate indicators, for a variety of reasons, are statistics of family law proceedings in the courts. In 1981, there were only twenty five petitions for divorce *a mensa et thoro* (legal separation), two less than in 1980. These statistics are, or course, less than useless in giving an indication of the incidence of marriage breakdown, since this particular proceeding serves almost no purpose, having been replaced in practical terms by other remedies, including maintenance and guardianship proceedings. In 1981, twenty-one petitions were issued in the High Court for nullity of marriage; eight decrees were granted. These statistics - again negligible in number - would suggest that civil nullity proceedings are not at present generally perceived by spouses or their legal advisers as affording an easy way around the ban on divorce. (Cost considerations would also, of course, be an important factor.)

Maintenance proceedings throw some more light on the incidence of marriage breakdown, but unfortunately they are less useful in helping us determine the extent to which marriage breakdown may have been increasing over the years. This is because before 1976 the maintenance legislation was a relatively antiquated procedure, to which many spouses were clearly not inclined to resort. In that year the legislation was placed on a modern footing, with expanded procedures of enforcement and collection. Coupled with the growth of legal aid – pioneered by law students over a decade ago - maintenance proceedings became a more attractive option. In a period of just under four years from 1976 to 1980, over three thousand maintenance summonses were issued.

Proceedings relating to the custody and welfare of children, taken under the *Guardianship of Infants Act 1964,* increased from 211 in 1978 to 295 in 1979.

Interesting though these legal statistics are, they suffer from a number of limitations as indicators of the incidence or growth of marriage breakdown. Clearly many spouses whose marriages have broken down do not resort to court proceedings; conversely it is not inconceivable that a certain number of couples involved in maintenance or custody proceedings are not finally estranged. Moreover, as already mentioned, such factors as the availability or otherwise of legal aid must be taken into consideration. One has only to refer to the writings of Professor Oliver McGregor in England to be reminded of how cautious we should be in drawing any confident inference from changes in the statistics of judicial proceedings.

The statistics regarding social welfare payments to deserted wives are a more useful guide. The combined number of recipients of the Deserted Wife's Allowance and the Deserted Wife's Benefit rose by just over 1500 from 5168 in 1977 to 6698 in 1982. These statistics do not, of course, take account of deserted husbands, couples who have separated by consent, and those wives who do not qualify, or do not apply, for the Allowance or Benefit. On the other side of the coin, it seems reasonable to assume that not all recipients have finally separated from their husbands: this is a matter on which empirical evidence (even by means of a limited study) would be relatively easy to obtain.

We must also take into account the broken marriages of the several thousands of couples who, one may presume, never find themselves counted in the social welfare or judicial statistics. Unfortunately their number is as yet a matter of speculation.

Returning, therefore, to our hypothetical society and contrasting with our present society, can we say that the evidence es-

tablishes that our present society has replaced the norm of permanence in relationships by a norm of impermanence? Has the
notion of marriage as involving lifelong responsibilities between
spouses still general support or do most people reject this notion
as obsolete? Experience would suggest the norm of marriage as
involving the undertaking of lifelong responsibilities has not yet
been replaced in our community. This does not mean that some
marriages do not break down. Nor does it suggest that many
members of our society are willing to show compassion towards
those whose marriages have resulted in separation: indeed
public opinion surveys taken over the years indicate increasing
willingness on the part of our community to contemplate divorce
as a solution for the problem of marriage breakdown. But there
is little evidence of a general rejection of the notion of marriage
as involving lifelong responsibilities, or of rejection of the norm of
permanence in commitment in marriage. It would be wrong to
interpret a humanitarian and compassionate concern for those
whose marriages have broken down as evidence of a rejection of
the norms on which marriage is based.

Individual autonomy and the right to divorce

In confronting the issue of divorce, we must face a potential conflict between responsibilities and rights, between concern for the
welfare of others and concern for one's own autonomy. We have
already considered some aspects of this problem in our discussion of consensual divorce, where the wishes of certain couples
conflict with the interests of others. In the present context we
must consider the position of an individual spouse who wishes to
have a divorce. Why should his or her wishes be frustrated? Has
not a spouse the right to withdraw from a harmful and damaging
marriage? Why should the law coerce a spouse to stay married
against his or her will? Does this not raise an important question
of infringement of individual rights?

The response to this argument is that it would be wrong to
have regard only to the desires of a spouse or spouses wishing to
be divorced: we must also consider the interests of *other* persons
- spouses and children - who would be damaged by the introduction of divorce. What would liberate one spouse would frequently restrict the autonomy and rights of another spouse. We are
faced with a task of balancing interests, which must have concern for the individual rights, not only of those who believe that
they would benefit from being divorced but also of those who
would suffer detriment as a result of the introduction of divorce.

Is divorce the answer?

It seems, therefore, that on balance divorce is not the answer to the problem of marriage disruption. We have seen that the experience of other countries is that the promises of the proponents of divorce have been substantially unfulfilled. The radical experiment of no-fault divorce, which has virtually swept the world in recent years, is only now coming to its fruition. In Ireland we are in the fortunate position that we have not yet committed ourselves to a path from which, in practical social terms, there is likely to be no return. We should learn from the experience of other countries over the next few years as the full implications of the experiment with divorce gradually unfold.

CHAPTER 13

Directions of Possible Reform

If divorce is not an acceptable law reform, this should not be the end of the discussion about the legal response to marriage breakdown: rather should it be the beginning. A society which says no to divorce is under a serious obligation to devise social and legal policies to respond to the problem of marriage breakdown. A considerable amount can be done both in the area of family law reform and more generally in the areas of social and economic policy to encourage marriage stability, to bring justice into all aspects of the relationship between husband and wife and between parent and child, and to mitigate the damage caused by marital unhappiness and breakdown. The problem will not go away, nor will all of the hardship and unhappiness be removed; but the position should, so far as is humanly possible, be improved. Let us examine some of these areas. Our analysis will confirm that many of the supposed legal advantages associated with divorce have no *necessary* connection with divorce and, in fact, in many respects can operate more effectively when the shadow of divorce is removed.

Matrimonial property

Let us begin with the subject of matrimonial property. Under existing law there is a system of 'separate property' in operation. This means that, as a general principle, each spouse owns his or her own property separately, rather than jointly with the other spouse. There are some exceptions to this rule. Succession law is an example.

As we have seen, the *Succession Act 1965* confers important rights on either spouse in the estate of the other when the marriage partner dies. During their lifetime, however, the general position is that, unless one spouse has contributed to the purchase of property by the other, he or she will not have an interest in it. In the context of the family home the results of this approach are particularly harsh. Unless she has contributed money to its purchase, the wife will generally not acquire any proprietary interest in the home. As Finlay P. stated in the High Court decision of *R.K. v M.K.* in 1978:

> the extent of [the wife's] work in the household and in the care of her children was very considerable but our law does not recognise so far at least a right arising from that type of work to a part ownership of any family or marriage property.

The situation was extremely prejudical to the wife before 1976. As has been mentioned, a husband could sell the home over his wife's head. The first news the wife might have of the sale was when the new owners arrived to take possession of the house. The *Family Home Protection Act* of 1976 prohibited the sale, mortgage or any other disposition by one spouse without the prior consent of the other. This has effectively resolved this problem, but the problem of the wife's lack of a proprietary interest in the property remains.

A variety of possible solutions may be considered. These range from joint ownership of the family home through systems of 'deferred community of property' – where the spouses do not share each other's property unless a Court has made an order requiring them to do so – to 'absolute' community of property, where spouses share all assets and liabilities in relation to property that is acquired after marriage or (in some cases) even property that was acquired before marriage.

It seems desirable for the law to encourage the spouses to regard themselves as partners in their property relationship as well as in their personal relationship. A knowledge that the home and its belongings are shared may provide a sound and encouraging basis for married life. Accordingly, it seems desirable that some form of community of property be introduced in this country. Its precise scope is a matter for discussion, but, at a minimum, it should confer on both spouses joint ownership of the family home.

It is interesting to note that the ideology of no-fault divorce is opposed to this community of property approach. The trend in the more advanced systems of no-fault divorce, such as Sweden and Denmark, is towards legislation dismantling provisions for shared property between spouses and replacing them by separate property regimes. This trend is entirely consistent with the philosophy of no-fault divorce. Thus, for example, Angelo and Atkin, speaking of recent legislation in New Zealand, state that it

> recognises that at breakdown a universal community is not generally acceptable, and that the presence and wise use of divorce laws create demands for a regime of separation of property.

Supporters of no-fault divorce argue that spouses should be treated as strangers after divorce: on this approach, as we have seen, the husband should not owe a continuing duty of maintenance towards his divorced wife. It may seem inconsistent with this view that he should be required to hand over half of his assets to a woman whom he can now regard as a stranger.

Moreover, since no-fault divorce considers that the divorced husband's future life is a matter for himself to determine, without concern for his former wife, then the likelihood of his remarrying must also be considered. Accordingly, from the standpoint of no-fault divorce, obligations to a previous spouse should not stand in the way of a satisfactory second marriage. But how is the man to afford a home, for example, in the same style as he was accustomed to in his first marriage if the community of property principle prevails? Certainly a system of community serves the principles of no-fault divorce less effectively in this regard than does a system of separation of property.

Maintenance of spouses and children

Prior to 1976, the law relating to maintenance of spouses was contained in a British statute enacted ninety years previously. This gave a married woman a right to sue her husband for maintenance only where he had deserted her. The 1976 Act modernised the law in a number of respects. Desertion was no longer the basis of an order for maintenance: henceforth it was sufficient to show that the respondent spouse had failed to provide proper maintenance for the family. This means that an order for maintenance may be made not only where spouses are living apart but also where the spouses are continuing to live with each other. The former law was an inducement to spouses to separate, since they could be awarded maintenance only after separation.

The 1976 Act also created a new machinery of attachment of earnings for enforcing maintenance orders, designed to provide an alternative in certain cases to imprisonment as a sanction for failure to comply with a maintenance order.

The Act reflects the recommendations of many persons and groups who, during the previous years, had expressed concern for the deserted and unsupported wife. It was not presented as the last word on the subject, according to the Minister for Justice when introducing it to the Oireachtas. So, what further changes in the law might be desirable? Let us examine some possible avenues of further reform.

First (adopting a suggestion made by Ms Pam Lynch, AIM Administrator) the machinery for the attachment of earnings of those who do not comply with maintenance orders should be extended to proprietors of businesses and shareholders. The present form of attachment of earnings system cannot be applied to such persons, since there is no salary or wage to attach, but a modified system of periodical deductions could be devised to cover these cases. Such an improved system would be in the interest of the wife, since it would remove the need for imprisonment for non-compliance with a court order for maintenance – a solution that benefits neither her nor her defaulting husband.

Secondly, the Court should be given wider powers than under the present law to make financial orders. At present, the Court may order only periodical payments of maintenance: it cannot order the payment of a lump sum, for example. Several commentators have criticised this lacuna. An expansion of powers here would appear desirable.

Thirdly, the law should impose an obligation on spouses to disclose to each other how much they earn in their employment, and how much their assets are worth. The absence of such an obligation has been criticised by many organisations and commentators.

Illegitimacy

One area of our family law that has come under criticism in recent years is the concept of illegitimacy of children.

Illegitimacy carries with it a number of important legal consequences. While the child's right to be maintained by his or her parents is substantially the same as that of a child born within marriage, there are some significant differences. The child's succession rights are far more limited than those of a child born within marriage. Moreover, his or her mother is the sole guardian, in contrast to a child born within marriage, both of whose parents are joint guardians. Another important difference relates to the constitutional area, where the father of a child born outside marriage does not have the rights conferred by the Constitution on fathers of children born within marriage.

What approach should our law take towards the legal position of children born outside marriage? As has already been indicated earlier in the book, it seems that the proper approach would be to abolish the concept of illegitimacy. Justice requires that the rights of children should not be limited on the basis of the marital status of their parents.

In practical terms, implementing this principle of equality causes problems in only a few areas. There is no difficulty in equalising rights of maintenance and succession, in enabling the Court to make declarations as to paternity, and in entitling fathers to acknowledge their children. More difficult questions arise in relation to the guardianship and custody of children. If all children are to be treated equally by the law does this principle of equality apply to their guardianship and custody? If it does apply, this would mean that fathers and mothers of children born outside marriage would in all cases be their joint guardians. There are differing views on whether this would be desirable. From the standpoint of equality the change would be welcome : indeed no other solution would be satisfactory. But some feminist commentators oppose it on the basis that it would force on the mother a legal relationship with the father which she might not welcome. A possible compromise would be to limit paternal guardianship rights to cases where the parents are living together or the Court has made an order granting these rights to the parents jointly.

The Law Reform Commission has recently issued a very radical report on the subject, recommending the abolition of the concept of illegitimacy and equalisation of the rights of children, regardless of the marital status of their parents. This is the type of reform of family law which we need so urgently.

Marriage annulments

The present law relating to marriage annulments would clearly benefit from a number of important reforms. Perhaps the most important from the standpoint of children is the rule that, where the marriage is annulled, the children will be declared illegitimate. (Where the marriage is void, the children are illegitimate even if no decree declaring the marriage void is obtained.) As proposed already in relation to the general subject of illegitimacy, this particular problem would cease to exist if the status of illegitimacy were abolished.

The second important defect of the present law concerns the position of the parties as regards maintenance and property after annulment. The law today adopts the logical position that, if there was no valid marriage, the parties should have no rights or obligations relative to each other. But this approach can produce hardship and injustice in some cases. A better approach would appear to be to permit the Court to make orders for maintenance and property disposition in appropriate cases.

When we come to the *grounds* for annulment, the position becomes more complex, but one point should clearly be stressed: *the problem of marriage disruption would not be resolved satisfactorily by enacting legislation which had the effect of introducing what in effect is divorce under the same name of annulment.* Apart from the lack of honesty which such an approach would involve it would also lead inexorably to divorce. Sheltering for a time behind a semantic 'solution' would afford no answer to the problem of marriage breakdown in this country.

Bibliography

Background reading

Relatively little has been written in Ireland on the subject of divorce. International developments have made little impact in the legal journals of this country. Two books should, however, be noted, since they will provide the reader with a good deal of information, written from an Irish standpoint.

The first book is Alan Shatter's *Family Law in the Republic of Ireland* (Wolfhound Press, 2nd edition 1981). This is a magnificent textbook, setting our Irish family law in very clear terms. Mr Shatter subjects the present law to a critical analysis and does not hesitate to make proposals for reform where he perceives inadequacies.

The second book is William Duncan's *The Case for Divorce in the Irish Republic* (Irish Council for Civil Liberties Report No. 5). The first edition was published in 1979; a revised edition with postcript was published in 1982. Mr Duncan is a family law expert who has written widely on the subject and has played an active role in family law reform in this country. Unfortunately I found that Mr Duncan's best qualities were not displayed in this book which suffers from several logical deficiencies and inconsistencies. I reviewed the first edition of the book in volume 15 of the *Irish Jurist* at pages 361 to 366 (1980). Mr Duncan replied to my review in volume 16, at pages 186 to 189 (1981).

CITATIONS

Presented below is a list of works cited in the text, as well as some relevant materials from which information used in the text is devised. (A more extensive bibliography is contained in *Divorce: The Social Argument.*)

AIM Group, Report No. 2 - Legal Separation in Ireland (1976)

Angelo & Atkin, A Conceptual and Structural Overview of the Matrimonial Property Act 1976, 7 New Zealand University Law Review 237 (1977)

Barber, Divorce - The Changing Law, in Divorce, Society and the Law (1969)

Bates, Counselling and Reconciliation Provisions - An Exercise in Futility, 8 Family Law Quarterly 248 (1978)

Berkovits Towards a Reappraisal of Family Law Ideology 10 Family Law 164 (1980)

Bromley, P. Family Law (6th ed., 1981)

Bumpass & Rindfuss Children's Experience of Marital Disruption, 85 American Journal of Sociology 49 (1979)

Burbury Some Extra-judicial Reflections Upon Two Years' Judicial Experience of the Commonwealth Matrimonial Causes Act 1959, 36 Australian Law Journal 283 (1963)

Burtch, Pitcher - La Prairie & Wachtel Issues in the Determination and Enforcement of Child Support Orders, 3 Canadian Journal of Family Law 5 (1980)

Butler A Sole Ground for Divorce: An Examination of Recent Divorce Reform in England in Anticipation of Reform in Australia, 45 Australian Law Journal 168 (1971)

Campaign for Justice in Divorce An Even Better Way Out (1979)

Canadian Institute for Research Matrimonial Support Failures: Reasons, Profiles and Perceptions of the Individuals Involved (1981)

Clark, C. Coping Alone (1982)

Commission on the Status of Women Report to the Minister for Finance (Prl. 446, 1972)

Conway To Insure Domestic Tranquility: Reconciliation Services as an Alternative to the Divorce Attorney, 9 Journal of Family Law 408 (1970)

Council of the Status of Women National Women's Forum, Irish Women Speak Out: A Plan of Action (1981)

Cretney, S. Family Law (1982)

Cretney The Law Relating to Unmarried Partners from the Perspective of a Law Reform Agency, ch. 36 of J. Eekelaar & S. Katz eds., Marriage and Cohabitation in Contemporary Societies (1980)

de Bessonet A Suggested Move in the Direction of No-Fault Separation, 3 Southern University Law Review 31 (1976)

Deech The Principles of Maintenance, 7 Family Law 229 (1977)

Deech & Eekelaar Family Law, ch. 7 of H. Wade ed., [1976] Annual Survey of Commonwealth Law (1977)

Eekelaar Family Law and Social Policy (1978)

Eekelaar The Protection of the Child's Welfare in Custody and Care Proceedings, ch. 6 of F. Bates ed., The Child and the Law (1976)

Eekelaar Children in Divorce: Some Further Data, 2 Oxford Journal of Legal Studies 63 (1982)

Espanshade The Economic Consequences of Divorce, 41 Journal of Marriage and the Family 615 (1979)

Evatt, Watson & McKenzie The Legal and Social Aspects of Cohabitation and the Reconstituted Family as a Social Problem, ch. 39 of J. Eekelaar and S. Katz., Marriage and Cohabitation in Contemporary Societies (1980)

Fennell, N. Irish Marriage How Are You? (1975)

Fennell Goodie Mister Cooney Has Pinched My Best Lines, Irish Independent, 1 August 1975

Fennell, N. McDevitt, & Quinn, B. Can You Stay Married? (1980)

Finlay, H. Family Law in Australia (2nd ed.1978)

Finlay A New Deal for Family Law - The Australian Family Law Act 1975, Rabels Zeitschrift 41 Jahrgang 1977, 71

Finlay Australian Divorce Law and Marriage Conciliation, 3 Family Law Quarterly 334 (1969)

Finlay Divorce Law Reform: The Australian Approach, 10 Journal of Family Law I (1970)

Finlay Divorce Without Fault, 47 Australian Law Journal 431 (1973)

Finlay Family Law, Family Courts and Federalism: An Opportunity for Reform, 9 Melbourne University Law Review 567 (1974)

Foster & Freed Divorce Reform: Brakes on Breakdown? 13 Journal of Family Law 443 (1974)

Freeman Divorce Without Legal Aid, 6 Family Law 255 (1976)

Freeman How Children Cope with Divorce - New Evidence on an Old Problem, 11 Family Law 105 (1981)

Freeman When Marriage Fails - Some Legal Responses to Marriage Breakdown, 31 Current Legal Problems 109 (1978)

Freeman & Lyons Towards a Justification of the Rights of Cohabitation, 130 New Law Journal 228 (1980)

Futterman Child Psychiatry Perspectives: After the 'Civilized' Divorce, 19 Journal of Child Psychiatry 525 (1980)

Glick & Spanier Married and Unmarried Cohabitation in the United States, 42 Journal of Marriage and the Family 19 (1930)

Gray, K. The Re-Allocation of Property on Divorce (1977)

Green The Making, Variation and Enforcement of Maintenance Orders, 11 Family Law 136 (1981)

Hahlo, H. & Sinclair, J. The Reform of the Law of Divorce (1979)

Hahlo Reform of the Divorce Act 1968 (Canada), in Law Reform Commission of Canada, Studies in Divorce (1975)

Hansen The Role and Rights of Children in Divorce Actions, 6 Journal of Family Law I (1966)

Hayes Financial Provision and Property Adjustment Orders: The Statutory Guidelines, 10 Family Law 3 (1980)

Heasman, K. Home, Family and Community (1978)

Hoggett Ends and Means - The Utility of Marriage as a Legal Institution, ch. 10 of J. Eekelaar & S. Katz eds., Marriage and Cohabitation in Contemporary Societies (1980)

Holden Divorce in the Commonwealth: A Comparative Study, 20 International and Comparative Law Quarterly 58 (1971)

Holt Support v Alimony in Virginia: It's Time to Use the Revised Statutes, University of Richmond Law Review 139 (1977)

Irving & Irving Conciliation Counselling in Divorce Litigation, 16 Reports of Family Law 257 (1975)

Jackson Book review, 89 Law Quarterly Review 22 (1973)

Kirkpatrick The Family: Disorganisation and Dissolution, in D. Sills ed., International Encyclopedia of the Social Sciences, vol. 5 (1968)

Krause, H. Family Law in a Nutshell (1977)

Krauskopf Maintenance: Theory and Negotiation, Journal of the Missouri Bar, January-February 1977, 24

Larson Equity and Economics: A Case for Spousal Support, 8 Golden Gate University Law Review 443 (1979)

Lasok The Reform of French Divorce Law, 51 Tulane Law Review 259 (1977)

Law Commission [England] Discussion Paper The Financial Consequences of Divorce: The Basic Policy (1980)

Law Commission [England] Working Paper No. 76 Time Restrictions on Presentation of Divorce and Nullity Petitions (1980)

Law Reform Commission of Canada Report on Family Law (1976)

Law Reform Commission of Canada Working Paper No. 13, Divorce (1975)

Lenon Book Review, 14 Journal of Family Law 123 (1975)

Lentin, R. & Niland, G. Who's Minding the Children? (1980)

Levin Maintenance: The Law Commission's Discussion Paper, 11 Family Law 67 (1981)

Macleod & Murch Special Procedure in Divorce and the Solicitor's Role, 12 Family Law 39 (1982)

Maddox, B. Step-Parenting (1980 ed.)

Malcolm, B. ed., Divorce Law Reform in Northern Ireland: Matrimonial

Causes (N.I.) Order 1978 (1978)

Manitoba Law Reform Commission Report on Family Law: Part I: The Support Obligation (1976)

Marsh Lee What Really Happens in Child Support Cases: An Empirical Study of Establishment and Enforcement of Child Support Orders in the Denver District Court, 57 Denver Law Journal 21 (1979)

Martin, J. An Essential Guide to Women in Ireland (1977)

Messinger, Walker & Freeman Preparation for Remarriage Following Divorce: The Use of Group Techniques, 48 American Journal of Orthopsychiatry 263 (1978)

Morris, D. The End of Marriage (1968)

Murch The Role of Solicitors in Divorce Proceedings, Part II, 41 Modern Law Review (1978)

Murphy, C. Divorce Irish Style, Irish Times, 21 November 1975

National Council for One Parent Families Maintenance: Putting Children First (1981)

O'Higgins, K. Marital Desertion in Dublin: An Exploratory Study (E.S.R.I. Broadsheet No. 9, 1974)

O'Neill Divorce: A Judicial or an Administrative Process? 4 Family Law 71 (1974).

Parkinson & Westcott Bristol Courts Family Conciliation Service, 77 Guardian Gazette 513 (1980)

Poulter The Definition of Marriage in English Law, 42 Modern Law Review 409 (1979)

Rheinstein, M. Marriage Stability, Divorce and the Law (1972)

Sabalis & Ayers Emotional Aspects of Divorce and their Effects on the Legal Process, 26 Family Co-ordinator 391 (1977)

Sachs, A. & Wilson, J. Sexism and the Law: A Study of Male Beliefs and Judicial Bias (1978)

Sage Dissolution of the Family Under Swedish Law, 9 Family Law Quarterly 375 (1975)

Samuels The Child, The Broken Marriage, The Court and the Social Worker, 6 Family Law 85 (1976)

Scottish Law Commission Divorce: The Grounds Considered (Cmnd. 3256, 1967)

Seal A Decade of No-Fault Divorce, 1 Family Advocate 10 (1979)

Seidelson Systematic Marriage Investigation and Counselling in Divorce Cases: Some Reflections on the Constitutional Propriety and General Desirability, 36 George Washington Law Review 60 (1967)

Special Joint Committee of the Canadian Senate and House of Commons Report on Divorce (1967)

Stuart Cohabitation: Part I, 25 Journal of the Law Society of Scotland 7 (1980)

Turner Divorce: Australian and German 'Breakdown' Provisions Compared, 18 International and Comparative Law Quarterly 896 (1969)

Turner Retreat from 'Fault': An English Lawyer's View, 46 Nebraska Law Review 64 (1967)

Viney, M. The Broken Marriage (1970)

Vischer & Vischer Common Problems of Stepparents and their Spouses, 48 American Journal of Orthopsychiatry 252 (1978)

Wallerstein, J. & Kelly, J. Surviving the Breakup (1980)

Weitzman & Dixon The Alimony Myth: Does No-Fault Divorce Make A Difference? 14 Family Law Quarterly 141 (1980)

Westcott The Doctrine of Irretrievable Breakdown, 11 Family Law 5 (1981)

Westcott The Special Procedure One Year Later - A Practitioner's View, 8 Family Law 209 (1978)

Wheeler, M. No-Fault Divorce (1974)

Wilkinson, M. Children and Divorce (1981)

Wright, D. Testator's Family Maintenance in Australia and New Zealand (3rd ed., 1974)